THE OFFICIAL
CHELSEA
FACT FILE

Facts
Neil Barnett
Paul Roberts
Pete Collins
Mark Faithfull
Paul Dutton
Scott Cheshire
Ron Hockings
Carina Dell

Thanks to
Pat Askey
Kate Booth
Steev Burgess
Nicola Roberts

THE OFFICIAL
CHELSEA
FACT FILE

EDITED BY NEIL BARNETT

BOXTREE

First published in Great Britain in 1998 by Boxtree
an imprint of Macmillan Publishers Ltd
25 Eccleston Place London SW1W 9NF
and Basingstoke

Associated companies throughout the world

ISBN 0 7522 2488 3

Copyright © Neil Barnett

9 8 7 6 5 4 3 2 1

A CIP catalogue record for this book is available from
the British Library.

Printed and bound by Mackays of Chatham Plc, Chatham, Kent.

Contents

1.

The Players Give Us Their Facts

Ed de Goey: 'I've been sent off twice in Holland. For Feyenoord against Vitesse I did nothing wrong. It was a one against one, I was coming for the ball, he jumped over me and tried to land on his feet but fell down. The referee gave a free-kick to him and a red card to me. Afterwards when it was too late it was changed to a yellow card.'

Dan Petrescu: 'I was a striker until I was 15. Now I'm a right-back or in midfield. I started up at Steaua Bucharest and for six years I was a striker. When I went to the Under-16s team, the manager switched me to right-back. That's why I like to score goals.'

Celestine Babayaro: 'I scored in the Olympic Final against Argentina. There was a cross from the right and I headed it in. I did a big jump, the double somersault and then some funny dancing which I didn't mean to. It just came. We won the gold medal.'

Frank Leboeuf: 'I worked with the French embassy about a tape, how to learn French from English: *We are Crazy about Football*. They are selling it to all English schools, and maybe we can see it in the Megastore.'

Steve Clarke: 'I once scored a goal in front of 95,000 people. It was the winning goal. We played in the Aztec Stadium in Mexico, Scotland Youth away to Mexico Youth, and we won 1-0. Pat Nevin took a corner, somebody flicked it on at the near post and I scored with a half-volley at the far post.'

Gustavo Poyet: 'I signed for the Uruguayan club Bella Vista but never played for them. There was a point in my contract saying if a European club came for me this contract doesn't stand. I was at Grenoble and one week later Real Zaragoza came for me.'

Gianluca Vialli: 'It is a fact that if you work hard at your game, in the end you get what you deserve. I believed it as a player, and now I believe it as a manager.'

Mark Hughes: 'I once hit a hole in one but I couldn't tell anybody. I was injured on a Saturday afternoon, Manchester United were playing Ipswich and at half-time were 2–0 down, so I thought, stuff this, and went off for a game of golf! Of course, I wasn't supposed to be there. At least I saved on a bit of money; I didn't have to buy everyone a drink afterwards.'

Dennis Wise: 'I played in the same school team as Les Ferdinand. He played in goal, he was a very agile keeper. He used to save them and now he scores them. I was in central midfield then, but I've only just got back there in the last few years.'

Michael Duberry: 'Michael Duberry made his debut against Coventry when still a youth team player and not against Leeds after my loan to Bournemouth which was 18 months later.'

Kevin Hitchcock: 'It's a fact that I can't stand cotton wool. It's a fact that I always beat Eddie Niedzwiecki at golf. And it's a fact that I had to look after Craig Burley.'

Graeme Le Saux: 'I was the first Channel Islander to play for England. I was also the last permanent signing by Ruud Gullit.'

David Lee: 'I once played in goal for the reserves. I went in for Roger Freestone against Crystal Palace at Tooting & Mitcham, and I was quality! The first thing I had was a one on one with John Salako and I smothered him. One went through my legs with the aid of a deflection. We drew 2–2 and I'd like to say I was outstanding!'

Roberto Di Matteo: 'You may know this, but I scored the fastest FA Cup Final goal at Wembley.'

Danny Granville: 'I scored two goals in my second game for Cambridge against Brentford. I played left-wing. I couldn't get a hat-trick because one of our players got sent off and I had to go to centre-half.'

Andy Myers: 'I used to be a centre-forward in my Sunday League side.

I knocked them in for fun. And then I was a midfielder. But Chelsea had me at left-back because I was the only one with a left foot, so I've been stuck there since. Until now, when I'm a left-sided centre-back. So I'm really six feet when I put my boots on now.'

Tore Andre Flo: 'When I was playing for Stryn where I come from in the Norwegian Second Division – like in England the Third Division – we won 12–0 and I got seven. That's my record. The club couldn't afford to give me the ball!'

Frank Sinclair: 'I made my debut in 1991 and in the seven years since I have had six managers: Bobby Campbell, Ian Porterfield, David Webb, Glenn Hoddle, Ruud Gullit and Gianluca Vialli.'

Paul Hughes: 'My first name is John. I'm John Paul. My mum always wanted Paul but I think John was to satisfy my grandma. My mum and dad have always called me Paul.'

Mark Nicholls: 'I broke my nose in three places at Wembley. It was the youth game against Luton before the FA Cup semi-final in 1994. The keeper punched me and it broke in three places and I was off to hospital.'

Dmitri Kharine 'I got an Olympic gold medal when I was 18 years old. The Soviet Union beat Brazil 2–1 in the final after extra time. It was 1–1 at full time.'

Eddie Newton: 'I was a prolific goalscorer when I was younger, playing for my school, Sunday club, my district. I was banging them home every day of the week. I played up front and midfield, but Gwyn Williams turned me into an out-and-out midfielder.'

Gianfranco Zola: 'I am very timid. This is a fact. People don't know it. It's my character. I have improved but when I was younger I was much more timid. Yet football on the pitch was another thing for me.'

Jody Morris: 'I've been with Chelsea since I was eight, ten years already. I had to train in the old car park shed behind the old Shed. Eddie Neddie (Niedzwiecki) used to call me Muscles because I was so skinny.'

2.

Five FA Cup Finals
and a Replay

A moral in the story? Chelsea have played in fewer finals than the teams who have beaten them: Manchester United, Spurs and Sheffield United. But they have played in more finals than the sides they have beaten: Leeds and Middlesbrough.

Chelsea have had a different manager for each of their Cup Finals: David Calderhead, Tommy Docherty, Dave Sexton, Glenn Hoddle and Ruud Gullit.

Five players appeared in the 1994 and 1997 Cup Finals: Eddie Newton, Frank Sinclair, Steve Clarke and Dennis Wise, as well as Mark Hughes who played for Manchester United in the first one . . .

. . . And two of them scored: Mark Hughes in 1994 and Eddie Newton in 1997.

Mark Hughes became the latest player to appear in five Cup Finals when he played for Chelsea in 1997. He also became the first to pick up four winner's medals.

Bobby Tambling was the first Chelsea player to score an FA Cup Final goal, but it was only a consolation as Spurs had already scored twice.

Peter Osgood's equalizer in the 1970 replay continues to make him the last player to score in every round of the FA Cup.

Glenn Hoddle became the first Chelsea manager to make an appearance as a player at the Cup Final when he came on as substitute in 1994.

In 1997 Ruud Gullit became the first foreign coach, the first black coach and the youngest coach to win the FA Cup as well as the first Chelsea manager to win the trophy at Wembley.

The 1997 Cup Final was also the least English affair on record, with 13 players from eight countries in the 22 man starting line-up.

The venue for Chelsea's first ever Cup Final appearance in 1915 should have been Crystal Palace but was switched to Old Trafford. That made attendance more difficult, thus limiting absenteeism by workers carrying out essential war work.

In 1970 Chelsea and Leeds stepped out on to the famous Wembley pitch to find it muddy and badly rutted. It had just hosted the Horse of the Year Show.

In 1915 Chelsea lost the FA Cup Final 3–0 to Sheffield United, then promptly got relegated. They were saved when the war ended and the top division expanded so they were included again . . .

. . . In 1994 the Blues were again involved in relegation drama. In their last League game before the Cup Final Mark Stein scored in the final minute to beat Sheffield United 3–2 and send them down.

In the 1970 Cup Final replay Peter Bonetti played for much of the match with a heavily bandaged leg. He couldn't even take goal-kicks but still ended up on the winning side.

Eddie Newton only scored once in the 1996/97 season, but he chose the 1997 FA Cup Final to do so.

Tommy Docherty finally got his Blues to Wembley in 1967, only to be faced by two Chelsea old boys, Terry Venables and former goalscoring legend, Jimmy Greaves.

Chelsea have also borrowed from their neighbours. Four of Wimbledon's Cup-winning team: Dave Beasant, Dennis Wise, Terry Phelan and Vinnie Jones, plus coach Don Howe, all went on to join the Blues.

The Cup Final has only been played at Old Trafford twice, in 1915 and 1970, and Chelsea appeared in both games.

Chelsea's 4–0 defeat in the 1994 Final was the joint-heaviest post-war loss. Brighton lost by the same margin in a replay in 1983 to the same team, Manchester United.

Seven players appeared in the 1967 and 1970 Finals: Peter Bonetti, Eddie McCreadie, John Hollins, Martin Hinton, Ron Harris, Charlie Cooke and Tommy Baldwin.

Fred Taylor in 1915, Tony Hateley in 1967, Tony Cascarino in 1994 and Scott Minto and Frode Grodås in 1997 all played their last ever game for Chelsea in the Cup Final.

Chelsea's 1997 Cup Final goals were the last to be seen live on the BBC, at least for the moment. It went to ITV the following season.

In 1994 Manchester United won the double by beating Chelsea. In 1970 Leeds came second in the League and lost to the Blues in the Cup Final and in 1997 Middlesbrough lost the Coca-Cola Cup and got relegated before losing to the Blues.

The 1915 FA Cup Final was the last to be played before the First World War forced the disbandment of organized football. It became known as the Khaki Cup Final.

When David Webb scored at Old Trafford in 1970, it was the first time Chelsea had been ahead against Leeds. It was the only lead to stick as the Blues won 2–1 after a 2–2 draw in the first game.

Chelsea striker Vivian Woodward returned from war for the 1915 Cup Final but refused to play because he would take the place of Bob Whittingham, who had played in his position during the Cup run.

The 1970 Final was the first Wembley clash to go to a replay.

What might have been – Gavin Peacock had already scored home and away to do the double on Manchester United in the League when he beat Schmeichel again at the 1994 Cup Final. This time the ball hit the bar and Chelsea lost.

Chelsea blamed a Chinese meal for their lethargic performance in losing

2. Five FA Cup Finals and a Replay

2–1 to Spurs in 1967. One of the players claimed the chop suey they had eaten had put them off!

Since the war Chelsea have played in two pairs of Cup Finals. In 1967 they lost and three years later they won. In 1994 they lost and three years later they again won.

Lest we forget, in 1997 Roberto Di Matteo scored Wembley's fastest ever Cup Final goal, hitting the back of the net after 43 seconds.

3.

Gianluca Vialli

Luca Vialli is one of only four players to have won all three European trophies. He won the European Champions' Cup in 1996, the European Cup Winners' Cup in 1990 and 1998, and the UEFA Cup in 1993.

He has won 59 Italy caps, scoring 16 goals. He's played in two World Cups: Mexico '86 and Italia '90.

He was born to millionaire building developer parents in Cremona in Italy on 7 July 1964.

He was Ruud Gullit's first signing as manager as a free transfer from Juventus.

On his Chelsea debut at Southampton in August 1996 Luca hit the post with an overhead kick.

In his first 16 starts for Chelsea against Premiership opposition (including Cup games) he scored ten goals.

Despite losing his position as a first-choice striker in December of that first season with Mark Hughes and new signing Gianfranco Zola filling the two positions, he finished as top Blues League scorer with 11 goals.

His four goals at Barnsley on 24 August 1997 were the first Chelsea four-goal haul away from home since Gordon Durie in 1989; the first in the top flight since Peter Osgood at Crystal Palace in 1969; and his subsequent hat-trick against Tromsø made him the first Blues player to get two hat-tricks in a season since Kerry Dixon in the 1985/86 season.

Dennis Wise

Dennis Wise was Wimbledon's Player of the Year when they won the FA Cup in 1988 and Chelsea's ten years later when they won the Coca-Cola and European Cup Winner's Cups.

He did his traineeship at Southampton but left before the end claiming homesickness in spite of the fact that they were willing to offer him a professional contract.

He was a record Chelsea signing in 1990 at £1.6m and after lifting the European Cup Winners' Cup in 1998, became Chelsea's most successful captain ever.

In his second game for the Blues, away to Crystal Palace, he was sent off with Andy Gray in a flare-up.

On his England debut in 1991, away to Turkey in a European Championship qualifier, he scored the only goal of the game.

In 1993 Glenn Hoddle made him Chelsea captain and he remained skipper for all but three months in the middle of Hoddle's reign. However, when Hoddle became manager of England he was never selected.

Dennis became the first footballer in England to be contracted into the 21st century when he signed a long-term deal with Chelsea in 1995.

He was the special guest who jiggled the balls and drew the National Lottery in the week of the 1997 FA Cup Final. He subsequently lifted the Cup.

5.

Hat-Tricks

Early doors! In 1908 George Hilsdon became the first and only Chelsea player to score a double hat-trick when the Blues beat Worksop 9–1 in the FA Cup first round at Stamford Bridge.

The only other occasion two hat-tricks have been scored in the same game was in the European Cup Winners' Cup in 1971 against Jeunesse Hautcharage. Peter Osgood and Tommy Baldwin scored five and three respectively. Chelsea won 13–0.

Chelsea's most prolific hat-trick scorer was Jimmy Greaves with a total of 13 between December 1957 and April 1961.

After Jimmy Greaves (in descending order) are George Hilsdon with nine, Bobby Tambling and Kerry Dixon with eight and Peter Osgood with five.

Bob Thomson, renowned for having only one eye, scored a hat-trick in 1915 in Chelsea's 5–2 win over Swindon in the FA Cup first round.

Tore Andre Flo's hat-trick against Tottenham in 1997 was Chelsea's first against the White Hart Lane club.

Tony Cascarino scored three against Tottenham in the Makita Tournament in 1993, but as the game was not official his goals don't count in the records.

David Webb is the only defender to score a hat-trick when Chelsea beat Ipswich at Portman Road on Boxing Day 1968.

Kerry Dixon believes his best hat-trick was his last for the club at Millwall in May 1990. He scored one goal with his right foot, one with his left and one with his head.

By scoring three at Millwall on the last day of the season Kerry became the last Chelsea player to score 20 League goals in a season.

Wembley wizard! David Speedie is the only Chelsea player to have scored a hat-trick for Chelsea at Wembley. Chelsea beat Manchester City 5–4 in the Full Members' Cup Final in March 1986. Only Stan Mortensen for Blackpool in 1953 and Geoff Hurst for England in 1966 have also scored major Final Wembley hat-tricks.

Jimmy Greaves and Roy Bentley both scored hat-tricks at Wembley for England while at Chelsea: Bentley against Wales in 1954 when England won 3–2, and Jimmy Greaves in 1961 when England beat Scotland 9–3.

Other international hat-tricks by Chelsea players were scored by George Hilsdon who scored four for England against Hungary in 1908, George Mills for England v Northern Ireland in 1937, Tommy Lawton who scored four in two of England's games in the 1946/47 season against Holland and Portugal, and Jimmy Greaves in Luxembourg in 1960.

Chelsea's first hat-trick was scored by Jimmy Windridge in their first home match in September 1905. Chelsea beat Hull 5–1.

Two players have scored a hat-trick on their debut. George Hilsdon scored five in the old Second Division when they beat Glossop 9–2 in September 1906 and Seamus O'Connell did so in October 1954 when Chelsea were beaten 6–5 at home by Manchester United in the Championship season of 1954/55.

Neil Webb and Gary Birtles are the only pair to have scored hat-tricks against Chelsea in the same game. Nottingham Forest won 6–2 at Stamford Bridge in September 1986.

One of the most infamous trebles to be scored against Chelsea must be by Rodney Fern when Rotherham beat the Blues 6–0 in 1981.

Since the formation of the Premier League in 1992, only Dion Dublin and Patrik Berger have scored hat-tricks against Chelsea, both in 1997.

Clive Walker's two hat-tricks were both scored early in 1982. Chelsea beat Shrewsbury 3–1 at Stamford Bridge and drew 3–3 at Grimsby three months later.

Leeds manager George Graham scored one hat-trick while he was a player at Chelsea. It was in November 1964 when the Blues beat Birmingham 6–1 at St Andrews.

Alan Dickens scored just four goals from midfield in 55 games for Chelsea, and three of them came in a 3–2 extra-time win at Bournemouth in the Full Members' Cup in 1989.

By scoring six hat-tricks, Manchester City have scored more against Chelsea than any other team. Everton, Newcastle and Portsmouth have each scored five.

The highest number of hat-tricks in a season is seven in 1960/61: Jimmy Greaves scored six of them, against Wolves (a), Blackburn (h), Manchester City (h), West Bromwich Albion (h), Newcastle (a) and Nottingham Forest (h) and Ron Tindall scored one against Newcastle (h).

Chelsea have scored four in a season on five occasions: 1906/07: Windridge 2, Hilsdon 1, James Robertson 1; 1934/35: Bambrick 2, Spence 2; 1971/72: Osgood 2, Baldwin 2; 1984/85: Dixon 3, Davies 1, and 1997/98: Vialli 2, Zola 1, Flo 1.

Apart from 1997/98 there have been three other seasons with three different hat-trick scorers. In 1906/07: Hilsdon, James Robertson and Windridge; 1912/13: Woodward, Whittingham and Ford; and 1968/69: Baldwin, Webb and Tambling.

Chelsea have scored hat-tricks three times against the League champions elect. George Mills scored one in the 4–4 draw against Manchester City in 1937; Jimmy Greaves scored five at home to Wolves in 1958/59, Chelsea winning 6–2 and Gordon Davies scored three against Everton at Goodison Park when Chelsea won 4–3 in 1984.

The longest time without a hat-trick being scored is just under six years. Kerry Dixon scored at Millwall in May 1990, and the next was Gavin Peacock's in February 1996 when Chelsea beat Middlesbrough 5–0 at Stamford Bridge.

On the occasions that Chelsea have scored their 120-plus hat-tricks they have lost only three times: Joe Bambrick at home to Stoke in 1935 (3–5),

5. Hat-Tricks

Seamus O'Connell at home to Manchester United in the Championship season 1954/55 (5–6) and Bobby Tambling at Sheffield Wednesday in 1961 (3–5).

In the Championship season Roy Bentley scored a hat-trick against Newcastle. Chelsea won 4–3.

On the way to winning the FA Cup in 1970 Peter Osgood scored a hat-trick at Loftus Road when Chelsea beat QPR 4–2 in the quarter-finals.

Lee Frost, who only played 15 games for Chelsea, scored a hat-trick at Brisbane Road in November 1979 in the old Second Division. Chelsea beat Orient 7–3.

Gary Bannister scored two hat-tricks in just over a year; in QPR's wins over Chelsea in March 1986 (6–0) and September 1987 (3–1).

6.

European Glory in the Cup Winners' Cup

Clean sheet man Peter Bonetti conceded just five goals in ten European Cup Winners' Cup games.

Erland Johnsen was Chelsea's only ever-present player in the 1994/95 campaign, even though a UEFA rule limited each selection to only three non-Englishmen.

John Dempsey received a three-match ban after being sent off in the first round, first leg match away to Aris Salonika in 1970.

Marvin Hinton's goal at home to Aris Salonika was his first in 196 games over a period of five years and five months.

Raoul Lambert and Gilbert Marmenout scored the goals when Bruges won the quarter-final, first leg 2–0 in 1971. Lambert worked as a metal worker and Marmenout as a P.E. teacher.

One of Bruges' three full-time professionals was Robbie Rensenbrink, the famous Dutch international.

Chelsea were just nine minutes away from going out of the competition when Peter Osgood equalized the aggregate score in the second leg against Bruges.

Had there been no further goals in extra-time then a play-off game would have been held at Stamford Bridge. Penalties had been introduced that season but were only used in the first two rounds, not the quarter or semi-finals. However Chelsea scored twice to win 4–2 on aggregate.

Chelsea's semi-final contest with Manchester City was the first all-English tie in the competition.

Chelsea drew a League game 1—1 at Maine Road, three days after the first leg of the semi.

Manchester City had won the previous season's tournament on the same night that Chelsea won the FA Cup in Manchester.

Chelsea won the home leg against City 1—0 with Derek Smethhurst's only Cup Winners' Cup goal. Chelsea had so many injuries that centre-half David Webb played at centre-forward.

Chelsea won the second leg 1—0 when Keith Weller's indirect free-kick was fumbled into his own net by City reserve goalkeeper, Ron Healey.

The only ever-present player in the 1970/71 campaign was captain Ron Harris.

The 1971 Final against Real Madrid was the last to go to a replay.

Chelsea won the replay 2—1 after drawing the first game 1—1. The matches were two days apart. Midfielder John Hollins was injured for the second game and replaced by forward Tommy Baldwin as Chelsea attacked more.

The Final and replay were not actually held in Athens as is usually reported, but in Piraeus, the main port in Greece.

The 21—0 aggregate victory over Jeunesse Hautcharage in 1971 was a record victory in European club competition. The record still stands (jointly with Feyenoord) today.

At 160 pages, the programme for the game in Hautcharage is the largest ever produced for a Chelsea game.

The village of Hautcharage had a population of 704 when they won the Luxembourg Cup. A local brewery promised the entire village all the beer they could drink in three days.

The 8—0 win in the first leg is Chelsea's largest away win. The 13—0 home win is Chelsea's biggest win of any description.

John Boyle, Marvin Hinton and Charlie Cooke were the only outfield players to fail to score in the 13–0 win.

John Hollins missed a penalty against Swedish part-timers Atvidaberg in the next round. Ultimately it meant that Chelsea were eliminated on the away goals rule.

Scott Minto made his Chelsea debut in the match at home to Viktoria Zizkov in 1994.

After being out of Europe for 23 years, Chelsea scored twice in the first four minutes against Zizkov through Paul Furlong and Frank Sinclair.

The first-round second leg against Victoria Zizkov was moved 60km to Jablonec because of the poor state of Zizkov's home ground.

Bruges had moved home between the quarter-finals of 1971 and 1995. The first was played at the Klokke, the second at the Olympiastadion.

The game in Tromsø in 1997 was played at the most northern professional football club in the world.

Lee Carroll and Alan Judge were amongst the substitute goalkeepers during the 1994/95 campaign. They were both released without ever making a first-team appearance.

Graham Rix made two of his three Chelsea appearances in the 1994/95 Cup Winners' Cup.

When Chelsea won the Cup Winners' Cup in 1998 they became the first English team to win it twice.

UEFA keep a European Cup Winners' Cup League table giving two points for a win and one for a draw from the start of the competition. Chelsea's 1998 trophy-winning victory over Stockholm took them to 45 points in 17th position above Sporting Lisbon, Tottenham, and Sampdoria on goal differences, and one point ahead of AC Milan.

Roberto Di Matteo

The most goals Roberto had struck in a season before joining Chelsea was six for Aarau in 1993 when they won the Swiss Championship.

He was the Swiss Player of the Year that season.

Partly because he was brought up in Switzerland, he had received no international recognition before being capped at full level by Italy in 1994.

The midfielder was Chelsea's record buy when he signed for £4.9m in 1996.

He lived with his parents until he was 26 years old and left Italy for Chelsea.

His sister Concetta went blind when she was 15 years old. She was in the crowd at Wembley when he scored his record-breaking FA Cup Final goal in 1997.

His opening goal in Chelsea's 1997/98 European Cup Winners' Cup campaign against Slovan Bratislava was his first goal in Europe.

He is contracted to Chelsea until the year 2002 when he will be 32 years old.

8.

Gianfranco Zola

Gianfranco won the Italian League Championship and Super Cup with Napoli and won the Super Cup again and UEFA Cup while with Parma. In the UEFA Cup Final his side beat Juventus, who included his future player-manager Gianluca Vialli.

In his first international for Italy in 1991 he was partnered in attack by Vialli and marked by Norway's central defender and future Chelsea colleague, Erland Johnsen.

He was a long-time transfer target of Glenn Hoddle when Hoddle was manager of Chelsea, but Parma were then unwilling to sell.

In his first full month with Chelsea he became their first Carling Premiership Player of the Month. The month included an outstanding performance against West Ham.

Three months later in February he won the BBC's Goal of the Month competition for his effort against Manchester United. It was the first time a Chelsea player had won it for years. He won it again in April for his FA Cup semi-final goal against Wimbledon.

He became the first Chelsea player ever to win the Footballer of the Year award.

Gianfranco Zola's hat-trick in the 4–0 win against Derby in November 1997 was the first of his career.

Gianfranco is contracted to Chelsea until 2002 when he will be 36 years old.

Tait Robertson to Vialli: Chelsea Managers

Gianluca Vialli became Chelsea's first manager to qualify for Wembley in his first game in charge when Chelsea beat Arsenal in the second leg of the Coca-Cola Cup semi-final on 18 February 1998.

Three of Chelsea's previous four managers have scored the winning goal in Cup Finals: Glenn Hoddle (Spurs v QPR), David Webb (Chelsea v Leeds) and Ian Porterfield (Sunderland v Leeds).

Glenn Hoddle was Chelsea's second ever player-manager. In 1905 the Blues' first manager John Tait Robertson also filled both roles.

Dave Sexton and Gianluca Vialli are Chelsea's most successful managers. Sexton won the FA Cup and the European Cup Winners' Cup with the Blues. Vialli won the Coco-Cola Cup and European Cup Winners' Cup in his first three months as boss.

Ruud Gullit was Chelsea's first foreign manager.

David Calderhead was the first manager to take his team on a pre-season foreign tour. Chelsea went to Argentina in the summer of 1929.

David Calderhead is Chelsea's longest-serving manager. He joined in 1907 and stayed until 1933.

David Webb spent the shortest period in charge. He was brought in on a short-term contract in February 1993 and left in June when Glenn Hoddle was appointed.

Ted Drake became the first and only Chelsea manager to win the League with a side dubbed 'Drakes' Ducklings'.

Ted Drake became the first man to win the League as a player (with Arsenal in 1934, 1935 and 1938) and as a manager (in 1955 with Chelsea).

Ted Drake put an end to the 'Pensioners' nickname at Chelsea – he felt it was looking too much to the past.

During the Second World War Billy Birell became the first Chelsea manager to lift a trophy at the Empire Cup in 1945.

Tommy Docherty became the first manager to win a major knock-out competition for Chelsea when his side lifted the League Cup, but at that time it was still held over two legs with no Wembley final.

Tommy Docherty broke up his promising side when he discovered some of his players out late drinking in Blackpool. He later reflected he had been too harsh.

Former Chelsea managers Tommy Docherty and Dave Sexton both went on to manage Manchester United but neither could deliver the coveted League title to Old Trafford.

Between 1974 and 1981 Chelsea had seven managers: Dave Sexton, Ron Suart, Eddie McCreadie, Ken Shellito, Danny Blanchflower, Geoff Hurst and John Neal.

In 1977 Eddie McCreadie won promotion back to the First Division for Chelsea, only to quit after failing to agree personal terms with the club.

Danny Blanchflower came out of football retirement to manage the Blues. He was the club's first non-British manager but Chelsea plummeted under his guidance.

John Neal presided over Chelsea's worst ever season, when they finished just one point clear of relegation to the old Third Division. The next season they were promoted as champions.

John Hollins played for Chelsea in two FA Cup Finals, two League Cup Finals and one Cup Winners' Cup Final and was player-coach and manager at the club, all in two spells. The second ended with the sack.

9. Tait Robertson to Vialli: Chelsea Managers

Bobby Campbell is the only Chelsea manager to see the side relegated in the play-offs, though he nearly saved the team from the drop after taking over from John Hollins.

Bobby Campbell steered Chelsea to their most successful sequence of 27 games unbeaten. The Blues also smashed all the old Second Division records as they were promoted as champions in 1989.

John Neal and Bobby Campbell both won the Full Members' Cup with Chelsea (sponsored the second time by Zenith Data Systems).

Glenn Hoddle played at Wembley for Swindon to take them up to the Premiership through the promotion play-offs and then went back there within 12 months for Chelsea in the FA Cup.

Glenn Hoddle had spent six months with Chelsea before returning as player-manager. In 1991 he rehabilitated with the club after a career-threatening knee injury.

In 1994 Glenn Hoddle became the first Chelsea manager to take the Blues to the FA Cup Final for 24 years and the following season the first manager to take them into Europe since 1971.

Glenn Hoddle appeared in his sixth FA Cup Final match when he ran out for Chelsea. In those six games two were replays.

Three Chelsea players have also managed England: Ron Greenwood, Terry Venables and current incumbent Glenn Hoddle, who also managed the Blues.

Chelsea have had two international trophy-winning players as managers. Ruud Gullit won the European Nations Cup in 1988 with Holland but Geoff Hurst went one better when he won the World Cup with England in 1966. Ruud Gullit scored in his final against the USSR, Hurst went two better by scoring a hat-trick.

Ruud Gullit broke Chelsea's own record when he paid £4.9m for Roberto Di Matteo in 1996 and again when he handed out £5m to Blackburn for Graeme Le Saux in 1997. Gianluca Vialli then paid out £5.4m for Pierluigi Casiraghi in the summer of 1998.

10.

Ins and Outs of
the Transfer Market

In April 1910 Chelsea signed four players: Marshall McEwan, English McConnell, Robert Whittingham and Philip Smith, in a vain attempt to avoid relegation. It was because of this action that the Football League introduced the transfer deadline.

When Graeme Le Saux re-signed for Chelsea in August 1997, he became the first current England international to sign for the club since Reg Matthews in December 1956.

The £20,000 paid for Matthews was a world-record fee for a goalkeeper at the time.

The club record purchase of £5m, was for Graeme Le Saux, who had originally signed on a free transfer and was later sold for £625,000.

Chelsea's first ever purchase was John Tait Robertson in May 1905. He came from Glasgow Rangers for £50 to become the club's first player-manager.

Chelsea's first £1,000 signing was Fred Rouse from Stoke City in October 1907. He stayed at the club for just 16 months before moving on to Brentford.

The first £100,000 signing was Tony Hateley. He lasted just nine months.

A new British record transfer fee of £20,000 was established when Tommy Lawton left Chelsea to join Notts County in November 1967.

Alan Birchenall was Chelsea's second £100,000 purchase; he came from Sheffield United in November 1967. He later became the first £100,000 transfer out when he joined Crystal Palace in June 1970.

10. Ins and Outs of the Transfer Market

Chelsea's purchase of David Hay for £225,000 in July 1974 was the record transfer fee until September 1985 when Micky Hazard joined for £310,000.

Dennis Wise was Chelsea's first £1m purchase when he came from Wimbledon for £1.6m in June 1990.

Frode Grodås became Chelsea's first signing under the Bosman ruling when he joined from Lilleström in 1996.

Erland Johnsen and Scott Minto left Chelsea in 1997 under the Bosman ruling; Johnsen went to Rosenborg and Minto went to Benfica.

Ken Armstrong, a League champion in 1955 and Chelsea's record appearance maker before Peter Bonetti, was signed from army football.

Chelsea's biggest ever loss on a transfer is £1.45m. Robert Fleck was signed from Norwich City for £2.1m in 1992 and rejoined the same club for £650,000 in 1995.

When James Bradshaw joined from Fulham in 1909, he was sold by his father, then manager of Fulham.

Jimmy Greaves became the first English player to leave Chelsea for a foreign club when he joined AC Milan in 1961.

Muzzy Izzet left Chelsea for Leicester in July 1996 for an initial fee of £650,000; a Chelsea record for a youth team player without a first-team appearance.

The transfer tribunal fee for Kevin Wilson's move from Ipswich Town in July 1987 was increased by £10,000 when it was revealed that Ken Bates had offered Wilson an improved contract in a taxi returning from the original hearing.

Scottish international Alex Cheyne was one of the first Football League players to move abroad for financial reasons when he joined French club Nîmes in 1932. He returned to Stamford Bridge two years later.

The first ever signing from an American club was Alexander Donald from

New York Nationals in July 1930.

Andy Wilson joined Chelsea for a club record fee of £6,500 from Middlesbrough in November 1923 just days after playing for Boro against Chelsea.

The first £10,000 purchase was that of Hughie Gallacher from Newcastle United in May 1930.

Steve Wicks cost a club record of £425,000 when he was signed from QPR in July 1986. He had originally come through the Chelsea youth ranks before being sold to Derby County in January 1979.

The first purchase by Chelsea after Ken Bates became chairman was that of David Speedie, in May 1982.

Dave Beasant was Chelsea's first ½m purchase when he signed from Newcastle in January 1989.

Chelsea signed Dave Mitchell from Feyenoord in December 1988 on the recommendation of manager Bobby Campbell's son, Greg, who played in Dutch football.

Chelsea's first £1m sale was Gordon Durie. He cost Tottenham Hotspur £2.2m in July 1991.

When Chelsea sold Pat Nevin to Everton for £925,000 in July 1988, it was the record fee set by a transfer tribunal.

Ruud Gullit's first signing for Chelsea was Gianluca Vialli, the man who later succeeded him as manager.

In July 1983 a transfer tribunal fixed the fee for the sale of Mike Fillery to QPR at £155,000. It was £30,000 less than QPR had offered!

Cash-strapped times! When Duncan McKenzie signed for Chelsea for £165,000 in September 1978, he became the club's first cash purchase since David Hay in July 1974.

11.

Steve Clarke

Steve Clarke's first game at Wembley was for the Football League against the Rest of the World in 1987, a game commemorating the Football League's centenary.

Steve missed the 1990 World Cup in Italy when he returned with an aggravated back injury from a Scotland trip to the country to train and look at facilities. When he recovered, Chelsea manager Bobby Campbell didn't pick him and he lost his Scotland place.

Steve was St Mirren Player of the Year in 1986 and Chelsea Player of the Year in 1994.

He became Chelsea's union representative for the Professional Footballers' Association at the beginning of 1989 and has been in the role ever since.

Steve's brother Paul played for Kilmarnock in Scotland.

His sixth and last international was the only one he lost. Holland, including Gullit and de Goey who later both joined Chelsea, won 3–1.

His benefit game in 1997, at home to PSV Eindhoven, attracted a crowd of 12,978.

He scored his tenth goal for Chelsea on 18 April 1998 against Liverpool his 417th game. His ninth goal had been in his 196th appearance on 18 April 1993 against Queens Park Rangers.

12.

Frank Sinclair

Chelsea were 3–0 down within 20 minutes of Frank's debut in 1991 at home to Luton. He played left-back, and despite Graeme Le Saux being sent off, Chelsea fought back to draw 3–3.

In Frank's fourth game Chelsea lost 7–0 at Nottingham Forest.

On loan to West Bromwich Albion, for whom Bobby Gould was manager, he was sent off against Exeter for making contact with the referee and was subsequently banned for nine games.

He ended his first full season in the first team, playing in central defence, as Chelsea's 1993 Player of the Year.

After being deemed by referee David Elleray to have given away a crucial penalty in the 1994 FA Cup Final he showed his character by scoring the first goal of the following campaign at home to Norwich.

When Peter Beardsley was at the height of his form for Newcastle, Frank performed a perfect man-marking job at St James' Park as Chelsea claimed a 0–0 draw.

In the 1997 FA Cup Final team Frank was at right-back. In the first game of the following season he again scored the opening goal away to Coventry, and celebrated by lowering his shorts which, despite his long shirt, led to an FA fine of £750.

In February 1998 he won his first international recognition, getting five caps for Jamaica and playing both wing-back roles as well as sweeper. He then scored the opening goal in Chelsea's 1998 Coca-Cola Cup Final win.

13.

Agony and Ecstasy:
FA Cup Semi-Finals

Glenn Hoddle became the first Chelsea manager to win at Wembley in the FA Cup. It was the semi-final against Luton in 1994.

Tommy Docherty took Chelsea to more semi-finals than any other Chelsea manager (three) but he never lifted the trophy.

Chelsea have appeared in 13 FA Cup semi-finals, winning five times.

Chelsea's 24-year gap between FA Cup semi-finals from 1970 to 1994 was the longest in their history. They then appeared in two more in the following three seasons.

Only nine clubs have appeared in more semi-finals than Chelsea but 16 have played in more finals and 16 have also won the trophy more times than the Blues.

The Blues were a Second Division side when they appeared in their first semi-final, losing 3–0 to Newcastle in 1911.

Chelsea got to their first FA Cup Final by beating Everton at Villa Park in 1915. However, the Midlands venue has proved unlucky for Chelsea on many occasions since.

Chelsea have played at Villa Park in six of their 13 semi-finals but only won there twice.

Having lost to Sheffield United in the 1915 Final the Blues lost at their ground, Bramall Lane, in the 1920 semi-final. The score was 3–1 to Aston Villa.

If Chelsea had won their semi-final in 1920 they would have become the only club ever to play the Final at their own ground as Stamford Bridge had already been booked as the venue.

In the 1932 semi-final goalscoring legend Hughie Gallacher faced his old side, Newcastle, for Chelsea but ended up losing despite grabbing a consolation goal.

In 1950 Chelsea conceded a semi-final goal against Arsenal direct from a corner. The goal from Cox turned the match and Arsenal went on to score again and force a replay. . .

. . .Four days later there was just one goal in it and who should score but Freddie Cox. . .

. . .And in 1952 the same teams met at White Hart Lane only for Cox to score in another draw and then strike two more in the 3–0 victory replay.

Chelsea played in three successive Cup semi-finals at Villa Park in the 1960s, only winning the last one in 1967 against Leeds United.

In 1965 a John Mortimore goal was controversially disallowed and Chelsea lost 2–0 to Liverpool in the semi-final.

In 1967 Leeds had a Peter Lorimer equalizer from a free-kick disallowed in the last minute sending Chelsea through to their second ever Cup Final.

In the 1970 semi-final Peter Osgood kept up his record of scoring in every round. He completed the job in the Cup Final replay.

Chelsea recorded their biggest ever Cup semi-final win in 1970 when they beat underdogs Watford 5–1.

Chelsea's worst semi-final defeat was 3–0 by Newcastle in 1911.

North London is Chelsea's favourite semi-final venue. The Blues won at White Hart Lane in 1970 and Highbury in 1997 and went on to win the trophy both times.

Chelsea have only played two semi-finals north of Birmingham, and lost them both – at Bramall Lane and Huddersfield.

13. Agony and Ecstasy: FA Cup Semi-Finals

Gavin Peacock scored twice in the 1994 FA Cup semi-final to book Chelsea's first FA Cup Final date since 1970.

Chelsea are one of only eight clubs to appear at Wembley in the FA Cup semi-finals.

Chelsea faced their second highest ever goalscorer, Kerry Dixon, in the 1994 Cup semi-final. Dixon was playing for his home town club, Luton.

Dennis Wise has beaten Luton in two FA Cup semi-finals, once with Wimbledon and once with Chelsea.

Ruud Gullit and Gianfranco Zola are the only foreign players to score semi-final goals for Chelsea. Gullit scored against Manchester United in 1996 and Zola against Wimbledon in 1997.

Ruud Gullit scored as a player in the 1996 semi-final against Manchester United and was manager of the winning semi-final team the following season.

Mark Hughes scored a last-minute semi-final equalizer to eventually take Manchester United into the 1994 Final against Chelsea and scored twice for the Blues in their semi-final win in 1997.

In 1997 controversy surrounded ticket allocations for the semi-final when Wimbledon failed to sell out their allocation while thousands of Chelsea fans could not get tickets.

Arsenal and Newcastle are the only semi-final opponents Chelsea have played more than once. They lost to both teams both times.

Chelsea's two drawn semi-finals were against Arsenal in 1950 (despite going 2–0 ahead) and 1952.

14.

Harris, Wise and the Rest: the FA Cup

Chelsea have entered the FA Cup competition every season since their formation in 1905, with the exception of the seasons during the First World War (1915/16 to 1918/19) and the Second World War (1939/40 to 1944/45).

Chelsea have played 298 games in the FA Cup competition, winning 139, drawing 77 and losing 82.

Extra-time has been required in 22 of the replays. A penalty shoot-out has been necessary twice: once against Millwall at Stamford Bridge in 1994/95 (lost 4–5); and once against Newcastle United at St James' Park in 1995/96 (won 4–2).

Chelsea have met non-League opponents on 11 occasions, the last being in 1919/20 against Swindon Town, who were elected to the Football League the following season when the Third Division South was formed.

Chelsea's biggest victory was against Worksop Town on 11 January 1907 in the first round, when they went through by a margin of 9–1. The 5–0 defeat of Wigan Athletic in the 1984/85 season was Chelsea's biggest win in an away FA Cup tie.

The highest attendance recorded at any Chelsea FA Cup tie was the gate of 100,000 at the 1967 and 1970 Finals at Wembley.

The largest attendance at Stamford Bridge for any tie in this competition was the 70,123 who watched the third round tie against Tottenham Hotspur in January 1964. The semi-final against Arsenal at White Hart Lane in April 1952 was attended by 68,084; the highest figure for an away match on a club ground was reached when Chelsea played Tottenham

Hotspur in the fourth round in January 1957 and the attendance figure was 66,398.

In Chelsea's first season the club was required to play the preliminary rounds of the competition, meeting in turn, the 1st Battalion Grenadier Guards, Southend United and Crystal Palace. The last two were not members of the Football League then.

In the 1945/46 season, and for the only time in the history of the competition, ties were played on a home-and-away basis. Chelsea lost three of the six games in their three rounds, against Leicester City, West Ham United and Aston Villa.

Chelsea's longest ever tie was in the fourth round of the 1955/56 season against Burnley. Five games were played over 18 days and lasting 540 minutes with Chelsea ultimately winning 2–0 at White Hart Lane. The other games were played at Turf Moor, Stamford Bridge, St Andrew's, Birmingham, and Highbury consecutively.

372 players have represented Chelsea in the FA Cup competition. The most appearances have been made by: Ron Harris (64), Peter Bonetti (57) and John Hollins (51).

151 players have scored goals in the FA Cup competition. The leading scorers are Bobby Tambling (25) and Roy Bentley (21).

Hat-tricks have been chalked up by George Hilsdon (once scoring six goals), Bob Whittingham (who scored four), Bob Thomson, Joe Bambrick, Bobby Smith, Peter Osgood and Kerry Dixon (who also scored four).

Chelsea have scored 13 goals in the FA Cup from the penalty spot, struck by 11 different players. The leading penalty scorer is Bob Whittingham who scored three.

Ron Harris was Chelsea's first FA Cup-winning captain, receiving the trophy from Dr A Stephen, President of the Football Association (HRH Princess Margaret would have presented the trophy had the match not been drawn at Wembley). Dennis Wise received the Cup from HRH Duke of Kent.

15.

Michael Duberry

Michael Duberry played for Chelsea's reserves while still a 15-year-old schoolboy.

In his first year as a trainee, when the youth team coach was Peter Nicholas he accumulated 51 cautionary points through yellow cards and had to go before an FA Disciplinary Committee hearing.

In his second year as a trainee, when Graham Rix was youth team coach he made his first-team debut in the penultimate League game of the season, at home to Coventry.

In his second year as a professional he was loaned out to Bournemouth. The second month of the loan had a 24 hour call-back clause and Chelsea used that to give him his second game for the Blues, away to Leeds.

In his third game for England Under-21s away to Georgia, he scored the only goal of the match.

In his third year as a professional he suffered a snapped Achilles tendon and was out for eight months thereby missing the FA Cup win of 1997.

He returned to first-team duty at Wimbledon without a 90 minute game under his belt. He had made two 45 minutes reserve appearances.

When he won his European Cup Winners' Cup medal in 1998 half his face was frozen without movement or feeling from a condition known as palsy.

16.

Mark Hughes

Mark Hughes joined Manchester United as a midfielder and only became a forward in his first year as a trainee.

He had been a Chelsea supporter as a child and owned a Peter Bonetti goalkeeper's kit.

His four FA Cup winners' medals are the most obtained this century. They came in 1985, 1990, 1994 for Manchester United and in 1997 for Chelsea.

He has also won two Premiership titles, two Coca-Cola Cup winners' medals, two Charity Shields, a Charity Shield shared medal, two European Cup Winners' Cups and European Super Cup winners' medals, two PFA Player of the Year awards and one PFA Young Player of the Year award.

He scored the only goal of the game when Wales and England last met in 1985 at the Racecourse Ground, Wrexham.

His MBE, awarded in the New Year's Honours List in 1998, made him the first player so honoured to represent Chelsea since John Hollins in the 1980s.

The desire of several Wales managers to play him plus Ian Rush and Dean Saunders, means that he has spent much of his international career in midfield.

He once played two games in a day, turning out for Wales before flying to Germany where he was on loan with Bayern Munich from Barcelona, and coming on as a half-time substitute to help turn a Cup deficit into a win.

17.

Four Times Top Three

Chelsea's first top three finish, in 1919/20, came in the season after they were relegated. They were given a reprieve when the Football League decided to enlarge the top division by two clubs.

A crowd of 70,000 attended the Good Friday fixture against Aston Villa that season – a Football League record at the time.

King George V and King Alphonse of Spain attended fixtures during the season.

Top scorer that season, Jack Cock, was a regular performer at the Walham Green Music Hall, as a singer.

Chelsea lost just three home League games all season – to Everton, Burnley, and Bolton. They won all three corresponding away fixtures.

Chelsea lost 15 League games during the campaign, just two fewer than the previous season when they were relegated.

That season is still the only occasion that Chelsea have achieved a League double over Liverpool.

Two members of the first-team squad, forward Harry Wilding and goalkeeper Colin Hampton, had been awarded the Military Medal during the First World War.

Chelsea's championship winning points total of 52 in 1954/55 was the lowest ever for a 42 game season.

Chelsea managed just two draws from six home games in September and October in 1954. That run left them in 12th place, six points behind leaders Wolves, having played one game more.

Four own goals were registered on Chelsea's behalf in League games — a club record.

One of the own goals came in the 3–1 win over Leicester City in December. It was officially credited as 'Milburn and Froggatt shared own goal'.

The total aggregate attendance for league fixtures at Stamford Bridge was 1,014,352; the only time in the club's history that it has topped the million mark.

Peter Sillett scored six goals in just 21 League appearances, despite the fact that he was a full-back. His career total of 34 goals is a record for a Chelsea full-back.

The Championship was won in the penultimate game of the season, a 3–0 home win over Sheffield Wednesday. The champions were applauded on to the pitch by their final opponents, Manchester United at Old Trafford. The Reds won 2–1.

Chelsea were drawn against Swedish side Djurgaargens in the first round of the following season's inaugural European Cup before they were withdrawn by the Football League who feared that the new competition would create a fixture pile-up.

In 1964/65, Chelsea finished third with 56 points, a club record. It was four more points than they had managed in the Championship-winning campaign ten years earlier.

Four Chelsea players reached 15 League goals for the season, the only time that has happened in the club's history. The four were: Barry Bridges (20), Bert Murray (17), George Graham (17), and Bobby Tambling (15).

Chelsea were unbeaten in the first ten games of the season. This is a club record for the top division.

The 6–1 win at Birmingham City in December equalled the club's biggest away win in the top division. The record stood until the 6–0 win at

Barnsley in August 1997.

Chelsea were unbeaten in away games with six wins and four draws until 19 December when they lost 3–0 at Sunderland.

With five weeks of the season remaining Chelsea were top of the League, but only managed two wins and two draws in their final eight games.

Six of Chelsea's ten defeats came at the hands of Lancashire clubs. Two of the other four were inflicted by West Ham United.

In 1969/70, Chelsea lost just one League game at home all season to the team they beat in that year's FA Cup Final, Leeds United.

For the sixth consecutive season, the highest home league attendance of the season was recorded with the visit of Manchester United.

Chelsea played three League games between the FA Cup Final and the replay. They won 2–1 at Stoke City, lost 1–3 at Burnley and beat Liverpool 2–1 at Stamford Bridge to guarantee their third-place finish.

Chelsea gained just one point from the games against the two teams to finish above them, Everton and Leeds United.

The total of just eight League defeats is still a club record for the top division.

The first and last League games of the season were against the same opponents, Liverpool. This was the only time that has happened in Chelsea's history.

The most expensive season ticket for that outstanding season cost £21 for the West Stand.

Ronnie Hellström, Sweden's goalkeeper in the 1970 World Cup Finals, spent five weeks training with Chelsea during the winter.

Goalkeeper Peter Bonetti became the first Chelsea player to be voted as runner-up in the Footballer of the Year poll at the end of the season.

18.

The Inter-Cities Fairs Cup

Stamford Bridge hosted the first leg of the 1958 Fairs Cup Final when a London XI played Barcelona.

The London Select XI that played in the first ever Fairs Cup Final in 1958 included three players from Chelsea: Peter Sillett, Jimmy Greaves and Bobby Smith.

Peter Brabrook missed Chelsea's first ever European tie away at Frem Copenhagen in September 1958 because he was on international duty with England. John Mortimer could not get time off from his job as a schoolteacher.

The Frem goalkeeper was called Bent Koch.

The rules of the competition in that season allowed Chelsea to play up to three players from other London clubs – a rule which Chelsea declined to take advantage of.

Ville de Belgrade, Chelsea's second opponents, was the name given to the team representing Belgrade. In reality their team was made up entirely of players from Red Star.

Left-winger Mike Harrison scored Chelsea's first goal in European competition in the 3–1 win in Copenhagen.

The cost of club travel to the game at Roma in October 1965 was £20.

Terry Venables scored Chelsea's first European hat-trick in the 4–1 win over Roma.

John Boyle was knocked unconscious by a bottle thrown by a Roma supporter during the second leg.

The 4,000 crowd for the away tie at Weiner SC in 1965 is the lowest ever for a Chelsea European tie.

The captain of the AC Milan side played in March 1966 was Cesare Maldini, manager of the 1998 Italian World Cup team.

Eddie McCreadie became the first Chelsea player to be sent off in a European tie in the home leg against Milan.

Ron Harris called 'heads' to win the tie against Milan on the toss of the coin. The games had ended 2–1 to the home team in both legs and 1–1 at Milan in a play-off.

In Chelsea's first two European campaigns the linesmen came from the same country as the home team.

Chelsea beat Barcelona 2–0 in the home leg of the semi-final to level the aggregate scores. Both goals were own goals, by Torres and Reina.

Allan Harris made his only appearance of the 1965/66 season in the semi-final against Barcelona. He later became an assistant manager at the Spanish club.

The semi-final play-off in Barcelona was broadcast to a close-circuit TV audience of 9,008 at Stamford Bridge.

Chelsea's first-round tie against Morton in 1968/69 took place just seven days after Leeds United had won the previous season's tournament.

The Morton side contained three Danish internationals: Borge Thorup, Preben Arontoft and Bjarne Jensen.

The DWS in DWS Amsterdam stands for Door Wilskracht Sterk (Strong by Will Power). Their goalkeeper was Jan Jongbloed who later played in the 1974 World Cup Final.

Chelsea drew the first leg 0–0 with DWS despite winning 14 corners to none and being awarded a 19th minute penalty. DWS won on the toss of a coin after the second leg was drawn 0–0.

DWS lost their next tie 1–4 to Glasgow Rangers.

DWS are now a park side in Amsterdam.

19.

Frank Leboeuf

In the summer of 1995 Frank Leboeuf played eight games in the Inter-Toto Cup to help Strasbourg qualify for the UEFA Cup.

Strasbourg went on to the last 16 where they lost to AC Milan.

His 1997 FA Cup-winning honour was his first in the professional game.

Before deciding to sign for Chelsea he spoke to his close friend David Ginola, then at Newcastle, about any problems on settling into English football.

He was Chelsea's record signing for three weeks at £2.5m. Roberto Di Matteo overtook and nearly doubled him at £4.9m.

Despite being a sweeper, Frank scored four goals in his first seven games for the Blues, two of them from the penalty spot.

In his first summer in England the locks were changed in the flat he was renting on Fulham Road while he was on holiday and he was left having to live in a hotel with his family. They have since bought a house near Richmond Park.

Frank started taking penalties at his first club, Laval. He didn't miss one. He continued with Strasbourg where he scored all but two or three, each of which were saved. He never missed the target entirely. At Chelsea he has scored every one.

20.

Graeme Le Saux

Graeme Le Saux was spotted by Chelsea manager John Hollins when guesting for Guernsey against Hollins in a benefit match.

He won four England Under-21 caps and two England B caps in his first spell at the club.

In 1991/92 he topped Chelsea's appearance list with 50 including two games as substitute. He scored three goals.

In 1993 he was one of two players sold by David Webb in Webb's three months as manager. The other was Mick Harford.

Le Saux was valued at £625,000. He went to Blackburn where he won the FA Premiership and 20 England caps. Steve Livingstone moved the other way at the same time, valued at £150,000. He made one substitute appearance and was sold to Grimsby for £130,000.

Le Saux was re-signed in 1997 for a club record £5m. Apart from Danny Granville, who was signed as a squad player with an eye to the future, he was Ruud Gullit's only British buy.

His nickname at Chelsea has always been 'Berge', short for 'Bergerac' after the television series based in Jersey, where Le Saux comes from. No-one called him that at Blackburn where he was just 'Soxy'.

In his first spell at Chelsea he played 109 reserve games, scoring eight goals. In his first season back he did not play a reserve game.

21.

The Birth of
the Blues

Stamford Bridge Stadium was opened on 22 April 1877 to replace the Lillie Bridge Sports Ground and was constructed purely to stage athletics meetings.

It was 20 years later that a London Athletic Club official starter, Frederick Parker, had the idea, and the vision, to recognize the potential of the site for other sporting activities, and Association Football especially.

It was through his friendship with HA ('Gus') Mears and his brother, JT Mears, that the idea of Chelsea Football Club was to emerge.

The project was severely threatened at one stage in the autumn of 1904 by a tempting offer from the Great Western Railway Company to purchase the land for the development of railway sidings and a goods yard. Gus Mears almost abandoned the idea of forming a football club.

With Mears in a state of indecision, a meeting with Parker was interrupted by a vicious attack from his Scotch terrier dog, resulting in a nasty wound to Parker's leg. So calmly did the latter react that Mears was sufficiently impressed to feel that his friend would be a trusted and ideal partner with whom to proceed with the project!

In February 1905, Archibald Leitch, the well known football grandstand architect, was commissioned to build a 5,000 capacity stand occupying the length of the touchline along the eastern side of Stamford Bridge.

On the other three sides vast terracing was built up with material from the excavation of the Piccadilly railway underground line, as well as from the Kingsway Tramway tunnel.

Originally the planned capacity of Stamford Bridge was 100,000 – a figure almost certainly reached when thousands obtained forced entry into the ground for the visit of Moscow Dynamo in November 1945.

Chelsea's application to join the Southern League was strongly opposed by other London clubs, notably Fulham and Tottenham Hotspur, so Mears and Parker lobbied football clubs from other parts of the country for support.

On 14 March 1905 Chelsea Football Club held a vital meeting at which the decision to canvass for election to the Football League was taken.

The following month, on 14 April, John Tait ('Jackie') Robertson, a former Scottish international half-back, was appointed player-manager.

Prior to the Annual General Meeting of the Football League, Chelsea strengthened their cause by signing several established League players, despite the uncertainty of their situation.

On 29 May 1905 the AGM of the Football League took place at the Tavistock Hotel in London where the continuing opposition of other London clubs to Chelsea's cause was made apparent.

On the previous evening, with much canvassing taking place, Frederick Parker had the foresight to bribe the barmaid not to mix any alcoholic drinks in order to keep his head clear for the following day! 'No scotch-and pollies, my dear,' he is reported as saying, 'just dry ginger'.

So confident was Parker that he took bets of five shillings both with Gus Mears and manager Jackie Robertson that Chelsea would be successful and elected.

Remaining calm on the morning of the meeting he was in no way put out when Gus Mears said to him: 'I've a meeting in the City to attend this morning, you'll make the speech on Chelsea's behalf, Parker.'

Warned that his allotted time to speak was three minutes, but conveniently losing sight of the time, he ended his speech by thanking the assembly for listening so attentively and ended by saying: 'You will come to the conclusion that you cannot really refuse us!'

Chelsea were duly elected – without ever having kicked a ball in their short history.

During the summer Jackie Robertson made further signings, assembling an impressive staff of more than 20 professionals, as well as enlisting the support of several amateur players.

With the first words in Chelsea's first official programme: 'They're off', Chelsea's opening home match was a friendly pipe-opener against Liverpool at Stamford Bridge. One of the linesmen was none other than JJ Bentley Esquire, President of the Football League!'

More seriously, Chelsea's first competitive match had taken place against Stockport County at Edgeley Park two days previously finishing in a 1–0 defeat. A week later Blackpool, also away from home, provided the first welcome victory for Chelsea who scored the only goal.

On the following Monday evening, with a 5pm kick-off, some 6,000 attended the first home League fixture, a 5-1 victory over Hull.

Perhaps many would feel that Chelsea had really arrived when a crowd estimated at 70,000 (over double the previous best) attended the game against Manchester United over the Easter Bank Holiday weekend. Truly, the shape of things to come!

Ten campaigns after their first, Chelsea reached an FA Cup Final. It was 52 years before they would reach another.

22.

Last but not Least

Ron Harris made his last appearance for Chelsea in a 3–0 Second Division win over Oldham on 3 May 1980, establishing a huge club first team appearance record of 795 games.

Peter Bonetti made the last of his 729 appearances (600 in the League) in the last game of the 1978/9 season, at home to Arsenal. The teams drew 1–1.

Frode Grodås made his last appearance for Chelsea in the 1997 FA Cup Final. He made just 27 appearances, but won a Cup Winners' medal.

Another player to make his last appearance for the Blues in that match was Scott Minto, subsequently transferred to Benfica in Portugal as he was out of contract.

The last of Tony Hateley's 33 appearances for Chelsea came in the FA Cup Final of 1967 against Spurs. He was then sold to Liverpool.

The two other players to make their last appearances for Chelsea in FA Cup Finals were right-half Fred Taylor (1915) and Tony Cascarino (1994).

In his last game for Chelsea, at home to Nottingham Forest on 29 April 1961, Jimmy Greaves scored all four goals in a 4–3 win.

The last player to win the Player of the Year award twice was Pat Nevin – he won it in 1984 and 1987.

Tore Andre Flo scored a hat-trick in his last game for SK Brann Bergen before joining Chelsea in July 1997.

Erland Johnsen was made captain for the day on his last appearance for the club, a 0–0 home draw with Leeds United on 3 May 1997.

Chelsea failed to score in the last nine games of the 1980/81 season which constituted 848 minutes of playing time between the last goal and the end of the season. In fact, the Blues scored in only one of the last 13 games.

Chelsea have come last in their division on just two occasions: 1961/62 and 1978/79.

Steve Livingstone made his first and last appearance for Chelsea at Old Trafford, coming on as substitute for 35 minutes on 17 April 1993. Chelsea lost 3–0.

The last player to score more than 30 League goals in a season for Chelsea was Bobby Tambling, who got 35 in 1962/63.

The last player to do it in the top division was Jimmy Greaves, who smashed 41 in 1960/61.

The last time Chelsea won the League Cup, in 1965, the club did not even bother to enter the competition the following season because it was part of the Inter-Cities Fairs Cup.

In his last game for Chelsea (a 2–1 defeat at Everton on 5 February 1992) Ken Monkou was sent off for cuffing Peter Beardsley playfully around the head.

Kerry Dixon also played the last of his 420 games for Chelsea in that match, but he scored the last of his 193 goals for the club at Norwich City on 11 March 1992. Chelsea won 1–0.

Chelsea's all-time top scorer, Bobby Tambling, made his last appearance for the club as a substitute at West Bromwich Albion on 30 March 1970. The last of his 202 goals came at home to Burnley on 5 April 1969. Chelsea lost 2–3.

John Hollins, Chelsea's third-highest appearance maker, made the last of his 592 appearances during his second spell at Chelsea, on 12 May 1984 in the 1–0 win at Grimsby, which secured the Second Division Championship for the first time. He made his Chelsea debut over 20 years earlier.

The last player to break the 400-game mark with Chelsea before Steve

Clarke (who did it in the Coca-Cola Cup tie at Ipswich on 7 January 1998) was Kerry Dixon. He reached the milestone in a First Division match at Notts County on Boxing Day 1991. County won 2–0.

The last player to score five goals in a match for Chelsea was Gordon Durie, who did so at Walsall in the Second Division on 4 February 1989 – Chelsea won 7–0.

The last current England international signed by Chelsea before Graeme Le Saux was goalkeeper Reg Matthews in 1956. He never played for England again after arriving at the Bridge.

The last three Chelsea managers (Hoddle, Gullit and Vialli) have all been player-managers. Only one manager previously had taken the dual role, this was Chelsea's first manager, John Tait Robertson (1905–07).

George 'Gatling Gun' Hilsdon, the England international forward, scored his last goal for Chelsea the last time the club played Gainsborough Trinity in the League on 2 March 1912. Chelsea won 2–0.

England international right-half Ben Warren played the last of his 101 Chelsea games on 28 October 1911, at Clapton Orient. He was forced to retire due to an illness which eventually brought his premature death. A benefit match between North and South was played at the Bridge in April 1914.

Full-back Jack Harrow played the last of his 333 games in a Chelsea shirt at home to Darlington on 20 February 1926. Chelsea won 5–2. He had been at Chelsea since 1912 and won two full England caps as well as an FA Cup Final runners-up medal in 1915. After retiring from playing he stayed on the coaching staff, notching up more than 25 years of service.

Bobby McNeil, the last survivor at Chelsea of the 1915 'Khaki' Cup Final, made the last of his 307 appearances for the Blues on 4 April 1927 at Southampton. The game finished 1–1.

Full-back George Smith played the last of his 370 Chelsea matches (a club record at the time) at Sheffield Wednesday on 21 September 1931. Chelsea lost 3–2. He moved back to his native Scotland with East Fife.

David Calderhead's last season as manager was in 1932/33. He had been in sole charge of playing affairs since 1907 – a stint of 26 years.

Inside-forward and wing-half Harold Miller played the last of his 363 games for Chelsea at home to Everton on 26 March 1938. Chelsea won 2–0.

Scottish international full-back Tommy Law played his last game for the club that same season, at home to Blackpool on 26 February. Chelsea lost 1–3. He won two Scottish caps, both at Wembley against England, and was one of the 1928 'Wembley Wizards'.

23

Eddie Newton

Eddie Newton missed his first two opportunities to make his Chelsea debut. On the first occasion he thought he was given a day off after finishing a loan spell at Cardiff. On the second he suffered a broken arm a couple of days before the game.

He scored on his Chelsea debut at Everton in the last game of the 1991/92 season and again in his first two starts of the following season.

Just before Christmas that season he moved up to centre-forward with half an hour to go at Tottenham and scored both goals in a 2–1 win. He scored another as emergency centre-forward against Southampton on Boxing Day.

Moving back to the anchor midfield role he scored just three times in the next four-and-a-half years. The third of those goals, coming after a break of 18 months, was Chelsea's second in the 1997 FA Cup Final.

He has won two England Under-21 caps.

From 11 years of age he played in the same West London District Schools team as Frank Sinclair.

In February 1996 he broke his leg against West Ham, starting a period of two years in which he was plagued by injury.

He has called his son Cassius after the original name, Cassius Clay, of his only sporting hero, Muhammad Ali.

24.

Dan Petrescu

Dan Petrescu has won the Romanian League four times, the Romanian Cup twice, and a European Champions' Cup runners-up medal with Steaua Bucharest.

His Cup medal in 1989 was won after the son of President Ceaucescu stopped the game in the last minute after a Steaua goal was disallowed for offside. He said it was onside and the game should be awarded to Steaua. And so it was.

Dan's European Champions Cup Final ended in a 4–0 defeat in Barcelona to AC Milan, for whom his future Chelsea player-manager Ruud Gullit scored twice.

Petrescu scored Romania's winner in their last group game in the 1994 World Cup Finals against hosts USA, thus ensuring qualification to the knock-out stage.

He missed a penalty in the quarter-final shoot-out against Sweden at which Romania lost. He has not taken a penalty since.

When he joined Sheffield Wednesday from Genoa, Tottenham Hotspur were also trying to sign him. However, as Wednesday manager Trevor Francis could go to Italy and speak Italian to him, he chose Sheffield.

His nickname is 'Ledge', short for Legend.

In the summer of 1998 his wife gave birth to their second daughter whom they named Beatrice Chelsea.

25.

Division Two Promotions

Chelsea were promoted from Division Two at the end of their second season as a Football League club in April 1907, finishing nine points ahead of second placed Leicester City.

George Hilsdon scored five goals on his Chelsea debut in the opening match of that season, against Glossop at Stamford Bridge. He finished that year with 27 League goals, and is commemorated by the weather vane on the East Stand.

Promotion was clinched in the penultimate fixture, against Wolverhampton Wanderers at Stamford Bridge, with the final seven games producing six wins.

Five seasons later, and after two years back in Division Two, Chelsea again won promotion in the spring of 1912, behind Derby County who won the title on goal average. Again, Chelsea finished strongly, winning 11 of the final 15 fixtures. From 11 January they maintained their position in one of the top two places. Leading scorer was Bob Whittingham with 26 goals.

During that season Chelsea's founder, HA ('Gus') Mears died, leaving behind (as the official programme said): 'a monument more eloquent than any carved epitaph in Chelsea Football Club and Stamford Bridge which he gave to the sports-loving masses of London'.

Chelsea's longest ever spell of Second Division football (six seasons) was ended in April 1930. Christmas proved a turning point, after which the club lost only three of the final 24 matches.

Promotion was clinched on the final day of that season, at Bury on 3 May. Losing 1–0, Chelsea returned to their dressing room to discover that rivals Oldham Athletic had also lost, at Barnsley, leaving Chelsea two points ahead, albeit with an inferior goal average.

In the final fixture in May 1930, the LMS Railway ran a 'special restaurant car train' which left Euston at 9.20am. Return fare was 16 shillings (80p)!

A crucial personality in the 1929/30 promotion side was George Mills, an amateur centre-forward with Bromley. Scoring on his debut on 21 December, he ended up as leading goalscorer (14 goals in 20 games), while pursuing his career in a city office during the week.

Chelsea's manager in their third promotion season was David Calderhead ('the sphinx'), then in his 22nd year of office.

In 1962/63 manager Tommy Docherty steered Chelsea back into the top division in his first year in charge, and after the club had spent only one season in Division Two.

From October to Boxing Day 1962, Chelsea chalked up their best ever sequence of results (10 victories and one draw from 11 consecutive fixtures) to open up a six-point gap at the top of the table.

Between 26 December and 2 March only two League fixtures were played by Chelsea as snow and ice caused an almost total shutdown of football in Britain.

66,199 attended Chelsea's penultimate home fixture, against Stoke City at Stamford Bridge. Chelsea lost to the only goal of the match, orchestrated by Stanley Matthews, a mere stripling of 48 at the time.

Two wins, 1–0 at Sunderland (Tommy Harmer scoring his only goal for Chelsea) and a 7–0 victory over Portsmouth in the final match of the season at Stamford Bridge, seized promotion by 0.401 of a goal, from Sunderland.

Chelsea's promotion in 1977 was achieved against a background of debts of £3.4m with creditors agreeing to a 12-month moratorium.

No transfer fee was paid for any player during 1976/77 and, after a some-what barren December (one win from six games), seven victories and two draws from the final 12 games enabled Chelsea to finish three points ahead of Nottingham Forest in the final reckoning.

Average gates in 1976/77 topped 30,000 for the first time for five seasons with a much needed boost to finances coming from the 55,000 present for the Boxing Day fixture with Fulham.

Steve Finnieston was leading scorer in 1976/77 (24 goals), while captain Ray Wilkins was an ever-present for the second season in succession.

Chelsea's first ever Second Division Championship was clinched on the final day of the 1983/84 campaign, against Grimsby Town at Blundell Park.

Manager John Neal had virtually rebuilt his team during the summer of 1983. Eight members of the old guard had left and newcomers included such Chelsea legends as Kerry Dixon, Pat Nevin, Nigel Spackman, Eddie Niedzwiecki and Joe McLaughlin.

Kerry Dixon (28), Pat Nevin (14) and David Speedie (13) were the leading goalscorers in that sixth promotion season. Dixon, Colin Pates and Niedzwiecki played in all 42 fixtures.

Chelsea's seventh sojourn in Division Two in 1988/89 was concluded at the first opportunity. After a depressing start to the season with the first win coming in the seventh fixture, Chelsea romped away to win the Championship with 13 points to spare.

Kerry Dixon was again the leading scorer, ably supported by Gordon Durie (17) and Kevin Wilson (13). Defender Graham Roberts weighed in with a further 15 goals, 13 of them were scored from the penalty spot — a Chelsea club record.

26.

Oh No! Relegation

Chelsea have been relegated from the top division six times: in 1910, 1924, 1962, 1975, 1979 and 1988.

On only two of those occasions have Chelsea finished bottom of the table, in 1962 and 1979.

When Chelsea were first relegated in 1910, the team was beaten in 15 of the last 19 games.

In April of that season, Chelsea signed four players in an unsuccessful bid to beat the drop. As a result, the League introduced the last Thursday in March transfer deadline.

Chelsea's fate that season was sealed by defeat at fellow strugglers Tottenham on 30 April. Tottenham won 2–1.

Chelsea finished in a First Division relegation place in 1915. However, when football resumed after the First World War, the division was expanded from 20 to 22 clubs and Chelsea were reprieved.

When relegated in 1924, Chelsea were the lowest scorers in the whole Football League with just 31 goals. Andy Wilson was the top scorer with five goals in 19 games – a record low for a Chelsea top scorer.

Chelsea were relegated that season on goal average, having finished level on points with Nottingham Forest and 10 points ahead of Middlesbrough who had been placed bottom.

From early February onwards the Blues were never above 21st place in the table that season.

Chelsea scored only eight goals away from home that season, another club record low.

26. Oh No! Relegation

In 1950/51, with four games left to play, Chelsea were six points from safety in Division One and with two points for a win, were extremely unlikely to stay up. However, the last four games were won and the Blues stayed up by 0.044 of a goal under the old goal average rules.

Chelsea's 25 seasons in Division One between 1930 and 1962 remains the club's longest spell in the top division.

When relegated in 1962, Chelsea used 31 different players, and every position was filled by at least three different names during the campaign.

In that season, Chelsea never moved out of the bottom two from late September onwards.

Chelsea recorded no wins in the last 11 games of the 1961/62 season.

In 1974/75, the crucial match once again proved to be an away fixture at Tottenham. On 19 April, Chelsea lost 2–0 to their fellow strugglers at White Hart Lane and relegation became virtually inevitable.

Ray Wilkins, aged 18, was made captain for the first time for that fixture by new manager Eddie McCreadie.

Chelsea won just four games at home that season, the worst record in the First Division.

Chelsea were the lowest scorers in the division with 42 goals and tied with Newcastle as the highest conceders. Both clubs let in 72 goals.

The 20 points won in 1978/79, when Chelsea finished bottom, is the lowest recorded by a Chelsea team.

That season also saw a record low number of just five wins for the club. Only three of those were at home.

The 92 goals conceded that season made up the worst record in the entire Football League. Champions Liverpool conceded 16.

Chelsea used a total of 31 players that season.

Peter Bonetti made the last of his 729 appearances (600 in the League) in the last game of that season, at home to Arsenal. He made his debut in April 1960.

Chelsea's closest brush with the lower divisions came in 1982/83, when the Blues finished 18th in the old Division Two, just two points clear of relegation.

Relegation fears were only banished in the last two games with a nervy 1–0 win at fellow strugglers Bolton (one of only three away wins that season) and a 0–0 draw at home to Middlesbrough.

Relegated in 1988 via the play-offs, Chelsea failed to win a League match between 31 October 1987 and 9 April 1988.

In that period, 21 League games saw Chelsea pick up just 10 points.

Nevertheless, Chelsea did not slip into the play-off position (18th) until they drew at home with Charlton in the last League game of the season.

Chelsea lost just two matches at home all season, but won just two away.

The Blues lost just one of the play-off games; 2–0 at Middlesbrough in the final. Boro lost two of their four play-off matches, but were still promoted.

Chelsea are the only team to have been relegated from the top division via the play-offs since they were introduced in 1986/7. In fact, after Chelsea's demise in 1988 they were stopped and play-offs were limited to promotion.

Ed de Goey

Ed de Goey played in all Holland's 1994 World Cup games in the United States.

He played behind Ruud Gullit in several of Gullit's last internationals.

The two sat next to each other on the aeroplane from South Africa to Holland after the international between the two countries in honour of President Mandela. Gullit was guest of honour at the match while de Goey was outstanding in goal. Thus the move to Chelsea was conceived.

Ed de Goey won the Dutch FA Cup four times with Feyenoord.

Probably his best game in Europe was in the 1994/95 European Cup Winners' Cup at home for Feyenoord against Real Zaragoza. Victim of many of his saves was his future Chelsea colleague, Gustavo Poyet.

He cost a Premiership record for a goalkeeper at £2.25m.

In his first pre-season with the Blues he saved three penalties in a shoot-out with Newcastle in the Umbro tournament, eventually won by Chelsea.

In his first season he saved two penalties in the Coca-Cola Cup quarter-final shoot-out and made three crucial brilliant saves in the semi-final first leg at Arsenal, to help Chelsea to their first League Cup Final for 26 years.

His last minute tip-away in the European Cup Winners' Cup semi-final at home to Vicenza saved Chelsea's passage to the Final. An away goal would have meant victory for Vicenza.

28.

Tore Andre Flo

Big Tore Andre scored 15 goals in 28 games for Norway Under-21s.

He started his full international career wide on the right in a 4–3–3 formation and rarely had a sight of goal.

As soon as he was switched to the centre the goals started rocketing in, most notably a hat-trick in Saudi Arabia and two more at home to Brazil.

With his contract at Brann Bergen running out in October 1997, his club accepted a £2.6m bid from Everton. However, as Everton were in the process of parting company with manager Joe Royle, the deal broke down. As he approached a free transfer, Chelsea snapped him up on pre-contract and then bought him for £300,000 with three months of his contract remaining.

In his last game for Brann he scored a hat-trick and on the whistle threw his shirt to an adoring crowd. Brann won 4–1 and his brother Jostein got the one for the opposition.

Tore Andre scored within three minutes of his debut, coming on as substitute for Mark Hughes at Coventry and heading in Roberto Di Matteo's cross.

Ten of his first 11 goals for Chelsea were away from home, including a hat-trick at Tottenham and both goals in the crucial 2–1 European Cup Winners' Cup quarter-final win at Real Betis.

He received one vote for FIFA World Player of the Year in 1997, from Azerbaijan against whom he had scored for Norway. They placed him first, Ronaldo of Inter Milan second and Ryan Giggs of Manchester United third.

29.

Serving their Country

Ray Wilkins is Chelsea's most capped player for England. While with the Blues, Manchester United and AC Milan he represented his country 84 times. He won 24 of those as a Chelsea player.

Glenn Hoddle was capped 53 times, though never as a Chelsea player. However, there was press demand for him to earn a recall but when the England call came it was as manager.

Ruud Gullit inspired the Dutch to a 3–1 European Nations Cup win against an England side captained by Bryan Robson in 1988. In 1997 he got one over on Robson at Wembley once again as Chelsea beat Middlesbrough to take the FA Cup.

At the end of the Second World War Chelsea bought England centre-forward Tommy Lawton. The next current England player purchased was goalkeeper Reg Matthews 11 years later in 1956. He never played for England again. It took another 41 years for the next current England international to sign, Graeme Le Saux.

Overlooked? Shed hero Peter Osgood made just four appearances for England.

Overlooked? Kerry Dixon became the latest in a long line of Chelsea strikers to receive scant international opportunities for England. He scored four goals in eight international games but never became a regular.

Surely Britain's biggest. Bill Foulke kept goal for England and Chelsea in 1905, weighing in at 6ft 3in and 22st.

Chelsea's Scottish connection was underlined with three of the Scots' Wembley Wizards of 1928 including Tommy Law, Alec Cheyne and Alec

Jackson. Scotland beat England 5—1.

Apart from breaking a host of club scoring records, former Blue Jimmy Greaves is also the third highest scorer in England's history with 44 goals. He scored 16 of those as a Chelsea player in 15 games between 1959 and 1961.

Sharp shooter Greaves won 57 caps but missed out on the World Cup Final to hat-trick hero Geoff Hurst, who later went on to manage Chelsea.

Roberto Di Matteo missed the Italy v England World Cup qualifying show-down of 1997 through suspension but was picked for the two play-off games against Russia.

Chelsea had fielded sides four times with ten current internationals before Gianluca Vialli took over. He did it in each of his first three games.

In 1996/97 Chelsea had three international goalkeepers on their books, Dmitri Kharine, Ed de Goey and Frode Grodås, plus Nick Colgan capped at U-21 level.

But in the 1930s they had both the England and Scotland number ones, Vic Woodley (England) and John Jackson (Scotland).

Scotland and Chelsea forward Tommy Walker had to set the ball on the penalty spot three times because of high winds but still coolly struck home a Wembley equalizer in 1936.

Tommy Docherty was a former Scottish international when he arrived at Chelsea but it was his bust-up with England coach-to-be Terry Venables which led to the break-up of one of Chelsea's best sides.

Gianfranco Zola hit the headlines in 1997 when he scored the only goal at Wembley to give Italy what looked like a World Cup group-winning advantage over England.

One time Chelsea defender Mal Donaghy is the third most capped player in Northern Ireland's history, with 91 appearances. He won 15 of them while at his final club, Chelsea.

29. Serving their Country

Uruguayan international Gustavo Poyet is the first South American player ever to play for the Blues.

Tony Cascarino's amazingly long international career started in 1986 and was still going strong when Ireland were knocked out in a World Cup qualifier against Belgium in 1997.

Famous Chelsea amateur Vivian Woodward twice captained England to Olympic glory.

Tore Andre Flo scored twice for Norway when they recorded their shock 4–2 victory over Brazil in the summer of 1997.

Dennis Wise played a dozen times for England. He scored just once, when he scrambled the winner in a European Nations Cup qualifier on his debut against Turkey, maybe with his bottom, maybe with his arm.

Chelsea have had three of the five most capped players in Welsh history on their books: Peter Nicholas, Joey Jones and Mark Hughes.

Peter Bonetti never lived down his part in England's 3–2 World Cup defeat by West Germany in the 1970 Finals after England had led 2–0. Yet he kept five clean sheets in seven internationals.

Celestine Babayaro is the first West African to play for the Blues and the club's only current Olympic medal holder. He has a gold medal for Nigeria's shock Olympic win in Atlanta when he scored in the final.

Savo Milosevic's eccentric career at Aston Villa has nothing on Chelsea's very own Yugoslav, Petar Borota, who won 14 caps for his country and was one of the most unpredictable players in the club's history. Despite being a goalkeeper he often appeared in mad dashes on the halfway line.

Chelsea fielded a record set of players in the 1998 World Cup. Roberto Di Matteo, Tore Andre Flo, Ed de Goey, Frank Sinclair, Graeme Le Saux, Frank Leboeuf, Celestine Babayaro, Dan Petrescu, Brian Landrup, Albert Ferrer and Marcel Desailly formed the highest number of players from any club in the world . . .

. . .while the Scottish squad could boast a blast from the past. Ex-Blues

Tommy Boyd, Craig Burley and Gordon Durie all travelled to France. Ex-Blues Frode Grodås (playing for Norway) and Roy Wegerle (playing for the USA) also went to France in 1998.

Right-half Ken Armstrong made only one appearance for England but it was a good one, the 1949 7–2 victory over Scotland.

In 1914 Chelsea fielded surely their most accomplished international sportsman. Max Woosnam played for England, won four Blues at Cambridge and represented Great Britain at lawn tennis in the Davis Cup.

Roy Bentley not only led Chelsea to their only Championship but also helped England to qualify for the 1950 World Cup by scoring the only goal for England against Scotland.

30.

Captains in Blue

Ray Wilkins is Chelsea's youngest ever captain. He was aged 18 years and 217 days when he led the team against Tottenham Hotspur in April 1975. It was only his 29th first team appearance.

The two players to have captained Chelsea on the most occasions have the same surname; Ron Harris led the team 322 times, and his namesake John led on 229 occasions.

Apart from the Harrises, six players have captained Chelsea more than a 100 times in the League since the Second World War. They are Roy Bentley, Ray Wilkins, John Hollins, Colin Pates, Peter Sillett and Dennis Wise.

Dave Beasant (4) and Peter Bonetti (3), are the only goalkeepers to captain Chelsea since the Second World War.

Graham Roberts captained Chelsea in 66 of his 70 League games for the club, the highest ratio of any player.

Ken Shellito, Eddie McCreadie, John Hollins, David Webb and Ruud Gullit have captained and managed Chelsea.

Ron Harris captained Chelsea in 25 of their 42 European ties prior to the 1997/98 season.

Of the 1970 FA Cup-winning team, only Peter Houseman, Charlie Cooke and Ian Hutchinson never captained Chelsea.

John Bumstead captained Chelsea in just one of the 409 games he played for the club.

Charlie Cooke has played the highest number of games for Chelsea without ever being captain with a total of 373.

Ron Harris lost the captaincy after Chelsea were beaten in the 1972 League Cup Final by Stoke. John Hollins took over team captaincy and Eddie McCreadie club captaincy.

Joe McLaughlin lost the captaincy after the first League game of 1988/89 following relegation when he ripped off his armband and threw it away after being jeered by the crowd.

Erland Johnsen captained Chelsea for the first time in eight years at the club when he led the team at home to Leeds United in April 1997. It was his final game before returning home to Norway.

Ruud Gullit became Chelsea's first black captain when he led the team in the FA Cup tie away at Queens Park Rangers in January 1996.

Tommy Law is the only player to captain Chelsea in just one FA Cup Final. Ron Harris was captain in 1967 and 1970 and Dennis Wise captained in 1994 and 1997.

Willi Steffen became Chelsea's first overseas captain when he led the team for one game in the 1946/47 season.

The only player to captain Chelsea in every game of a post-war League season is Ray Wilkins in 1975/76 and 1976/77.

Jimmy Greaves captained Chelsea just once, in his last match prior to his transfer to AC Milan at home to Nottingham Forest in April 1961. He scored all four goals in a 4–3 win.

John Harris and Roy Bentley shared the captaincy in 1950/51, but were replaced at the start of the following season by Bobby Campbell when they missed the start of the campaign because of a dispute over their contracts.

Tommy Baldwin, Alan Birchenall, Johnny Brooks, Stan Crowther, Tony Hateley, Joe Kirkup, Frank Upton, Dave Webb and Keith Weller all captained Chelsea for one League game only. All were made captain for games against their previous clubs.

Peter Bonetti captained Chelsea in three League games; when he equalled the club's appearance record of 362, on his 400th game, and on his 729th and final appearance.

Roy Bentley captained Chelsea 41 times in the Championship season of 1954/55. He missed one game through injury when the team was led by John Harris.

Dennis Wise lost the captaincy temporarily after the famous fracas with a taxi driver outside Terry Venables' nightclub which led to police charges on which he was found innocent.

Mark Hughes first captained Chelsea on his first return to Old Trafford to face his old club Manchester United.

31.

Dmitri Kharine

Dmitri was the youngest person ever to play in the Soviet Union's top division when he made his debut for Torpedo Moscow aged 16.

When he was 17 he won the Soviet FA Cup. When he was just 18 he won Olympic gold with the USSR.

He also kept goal for the Soviet teams which won the European Youth Championships and European Under-21 Championships.

At the age of 20 he suffered a ruptured cruciate ligament and was out of the game for a year, spending most of his recuperation in Spain.

At his third club, CSKA Moscow, he was captain as they embarked on their European Champions' Cup adventure having won the Russian League. Later, at Chelsea, he captained Russia in the 1994 World Cup in the United States.

When Ian Porterfield was manager he arrived at Chelsea for a week's trial. In his first training session he was unbeatable.

Until he ruptured his cruciate ligament again in 1996 he had kept a remarkable 47 clean sheets in 131 games for Chelsea.

In 1994 he saved three successive penalties, all away from home: at Newcastle, Viktoria Zizkov in the European Cup Winners' Cup, and at Sheffield Wednesday.

32.

Kevin Hitchcock

Kevin was voted PFA Division Three (that's the old Division Three before the Premier League was founded) goalkeeper of the year in 1988 before leaving Mansfield for Chelsea. He was Mansfield Player of the Year in 1985 and 1986.

He won a penalty shoot-out at Wembley in the final of the Freight Rover Trophy in 1987 making two saves.

His first penalty save for Chelsea was in a League game at Wimbledon in 1988. The victim was his future Chelsea captain Dennis Wise.

He missed most of the first half of his first full season at Chelsea with a leg injury and then on his comeback in the reserves he ruptured his cruciate ligament and was out for another year.

He has won all his penalty shoot-out competitions with Chelsea: Ipswich at home in the ZDS Cup in 1991; Ajax in the Makita Tournament at White Hart Lane in 1993; Newcastle away in the FA Cup in 1996 and Blackburn at home in the Coca-Cola Cup in 1997.

In or out of favour? At the end of his best season at Chelsea, playing 31 games in 1991/92, he was out of contract and was not offered a new one. At the end of his second most successful season the following year, with a new four-year contract won once he had reclaimed his place, new manager David Webb sent him out on loan to West Ham for three months after seeing him play one game.

In 1994 he was the first recipient of the Chairman's Award for 'Unsung Hero' due to his attitude and performances when called upon after a long period on the bench.

At an auction at a benefit dinner for him after ten years with the club, Ken Bates bought Mark Hughes' donated 1997 FA Cup Final shirt for £10,000.

33.

Down and Almost Forgotten

Chelsea have spent 19 out of their 82 seasons of League football in the (old) Division Two of the Football League.

Chelsea were elected to the Football League in the spring of 1905 and spent their first ever season as a football club in Division Two, finishing in third place, 13 points behind runners-up, Manchester United.

Promoted in April 1907, Chelsea returned to the Second Division two seasons later, once more staying in Division Two for a further two years, ending up in third and then second place in the table.

Eight months after the outbreak of the First World War, in the spring of 1915, Chelsea were again due for a further spell in the lower division but were saved from relegation by the extension of the First Division by two extra clubs, and a proved match-fixing irregularity which favourably affected Chelsea's points total.

Chelsea's longest ever period in Division Two of six seasons, was between 1924/25 and 1929/30, the final positions being in turn, fifth, third, fourth, third, ninth and second. In those years only the top two were promoted.

Bob Turnbull established a new Chelsea club goalscoring record with a tally of 29 goals in Division Two in the 1925/26 season, despite missing six games. It has since been surpassed by Jimmy Greaves twice and Bobby Tambling once, and equalled on another occasion by Greaves.

Finishing in fourth place that year, two points behind Portsmouth and Manchester City, Chelsea failed to win any of their last five games (three draws and two defeats) after battling against injuries to crucial players, notably Andy Wilson.

33. Down and Almost Forgotten

Twelve months later, in the spring of 1928, a similar collapse occurred, with four defeats in the final five fixtures. Chelsea had led the field at Christmas.

Leading scorer in the 1927/28 season was Jimmy Thompson, better remembered as the Chelsea scout who unearthed a prodigious array of talent, largely from the East End of London in the late 1950s and 1960s.

Remarkably, Chelsea's gate in the spell of Second Division football in the 1920s never fell below an average of 27,846, ironically the figure in their promotion season. In an eight-day period in the spring of 1928 attendances of more than 50,000 were twice recorded.

Chelsea's return to Division Two in 1962/63 ended Chelsea's longest ever spell out of the top section of 33 seasons.

Chelsea's return to the Second Division in 1975/76 resulted in their lowest ever final placing in League football of 11th, up to that time.

During that season, for the first time, no transfer fee was paid for any new player because of the serious financial position, and the average gate of 18,956 was the lowest ever until then.

On 3 May 1980 with Chelsea in their sixth chapter in the Second Division, the Blues eased one point ahead of Sunderland, and into the third promotion place. Nine days later the north-east club belatedly finished their League programme with a win which condemned Chelsea to another season out of the top class.

Chelsea set up a new, and unwanted, record by failing to score in their last nine games of the 1980/81 season in Division Two (848 minutes playing time).

Attendance figures fell to an all-time low in the 1982/83 season — on nine occasions failing to reach five figures. Relegation to Division Three of the Football League was avoided only by a 71st minute goal, from 25 yards, by Clive Walker at Bolton on 7 May 1982. As a result, Bolton Wanderers were themselves relegated.

34.

A Cup's a Cup!

Chelsea reached the final of the FA Youth Cup for the first time in 1957/58. They beat Wolves 5–1 at home in the first leg, but lost the return 1–6 to lose 6–7 on aggregate.

Chelsea won the Makita Tournament in 1993 and the Umbro Cup in 1996 and 1997. On all three occasions they won the semi-final on a penalty shoot-out, against Ajax, Nottingham Forest and Newcastle United.

A different goalkeeper saved penalties in the shoot-out each time. Against Ajax, Kevin Hitchcock was the hero, Dmitri Kharine kept out Nottingham Forest and Ed de Goey did the business against Newcastle. Both Kharine and de Goey made saves from Stuart Pearce.

The 1986 Full Members' Cup Final produced record receipts for any Chelsea match to that date of £508,000.

David Speedie became only the third player ever, after Stan Mortensen and Geoff Hurst, to score a hat-trick in a senior Wembley Final when he hit three goals in the 5–4 win over Manchester City in the 1986 Full Members' Cup Final.

Chelsea's first appearance at Wembley came in the Football League (South) Cup in April 1944. They lost 1–3 to Charlton Athletic.

The first Wembley win came in the same competition a year later. Chelsea beat Millwall 2–0.

The goalscorers that day were both guest players: McDonald of Bournemouth and Wardle of Exeter City.

John Bumstead and Kevin McAllister were the only two players who won Full Members' Cup winners' medals in 1986 and 1990.

Chelsea won the London Victory Cup in 1919 without conceding a goal.

The legendary Manchester United manager, Sir Matt Busby, guested for Chelsea in the 1939/40 Football League War Cup.

Walter Winterbottom and Ron Greenwood, both later England managers, appeared for Chelsea in the 1942/43 Football League Cup (South).

Chelsea took part in three penalty shoot-outs during the seven years of the Full Members' Cup. They beat West Brom in 1985/86 and Ipswich Town in 1991/92, but lost to Luton Town in 1990/91.

Kerry Dixon is both Chelsea's record appearance maker and record goalscorer in the Full Members' Cup.

Chelsea won the Cross-Channel Cup in 1993 by beating Le Havre 3–1 at home and drawing 1–1 away.

Chelsea competed for the Prince Philip Cup when they faced the Italian Under-23 side at Stamford Bridge in October 1975. The two teams shared the trophy after a goalless draw.

Chelsea have competed for the Charity Shield on three occasions. They won as League champions in 1955, but lost as FA Cup holders in 1970 and 1997.

Chelsea won the Glasgow Charity Cup in August 1965 by beating a Glasgow Select XI 3–0.

Chelsea have played Norwich City for the Norwich Hospital Cup (in 1908) and for the Norfolk Invitation Cup (in 1980). On both occasions they lost.

The lowest post-war crowd for a Chelsea first team fixture at Stamford Bridge was the 3,849 who attended the Full Members' Cup tie against Luton Town in February 1991.

Stamford Bridge hosted the FA Amateur Cup on four occasions: 1907, 1935, 1946 and 1948.

Chelsea beat Floriana and KB Copenhagen to win the Festival of Britain Trophy in 1951.

Chelsea Youth Team won the Southern Junior Floodlit Cup four years in succession between 1959 and 1962.

Chelsea played nine games in the Anglo-Scottish Cup. The closest they got to playing in Scotland was one game at Brisbane Road, Orient.

Chelsea played Manchester City in the 1986 Full Members' Cup Final the day after playing a League game at Southampton. City had played away at Manchester United.

Chelsea won the Middlesex Charity Cup in four of the five years in which they competed and did not withdraw.

The only team to beat Chelsea in the Middlesex Charity Cup was Hayes in 1991.

Chelsea's opponents for the Guinness Soccer Cup, held in Canada in 1992, were Dundee United, Victoria 86ers and Victoria All Stars.

The Football League (South) Cup Final between Chelsea and Millwall was watched by a crowd of 90,000 – a record for a war-time club game in England.

The Full Members' Cup was the brainchild of Chelsea chairman Ken Bates.

The highest crowd in the history of the Full Members' Cup was the 76,369 who witnessed the 1990 final between Chelsea and Middlesbrough.

Stamford Bridge was the venue for the first four Charity Shields ever contested (1908–1911).

35

David Lee

David made his debut as an 18-year-old substitute at 1–0 down against Leicester in Chelsea's fourth home game of the 1988/89 season after the Blues failed to win the first three. He scored the equalizer and won a last minute penalty for Graham Roberts to hit the winner.

Although he played in midfield, his manager Bobby Campbell likened him to Liverpool defender Alan Hansen after his debut.

In his second season he was on the substitutes' bench at Wembley when Chelsea beat Middlesbrough to win the ZDS Cup.

In or out of favour? In Ian Porterfield's first season as manager David was selected just once. In his second, David played 32 times. In Glenn Hoddle's first season as manager David started just three games. In his last he started 36.

He was the second recipient of the Chairman's Award for unsung hero when, in Glenn Hoddle's second season, with relegation threatening, he came into the team at Easter after the best part of two years out and played every game to the end of the season as Chelsea's fortunes turned and a finish of 11th was attained.

He has ten England Under-21 caps. In 1991 he was a Toulon International Tournament winner with the Under-21s.

In or out of favour? He has had four loan spells, with Reading, Plymouth, Portsmouth and Sheffield United.

In a reserve game at Bristol Rovers in 1996 he scored with a free-kick from the halfway line, and in a home reserve game against Crystal Palace he scored from the edge of the centre circle in his own half.

36.

Andy Myers

Andy was the surprise Ruud Gullit selection for the substitutes' bench in the 1997 FA Cup Final.

He was Chelsea's second schoolboy to attend the FA School of Excellence at Lilleshall for two years. Graham Stuart was the first.

He made his debut at 17 years and 4 months in 1991. On his full debut the following season he scored against Liverpool. His next goal came five years later at Sheffield Wednesday.

He was Chelsea's Young Player of the Year in 1991.

At the age of 18, while still young enough to be in the youth team, he played left-back in the FA Cup quarter-final, a 1–1 draw at home to Sunderland.

Although a central midfielder in the youth team, he started in the first team on the left-wing and then dropped back to left-back. He played left wing-back when the sweeper system was introduced before dropping back to left of the back three in defence, and he played in the centre when a back four was re-introduced. He is 5ft 10in.

He was in the England Youth team which reached the quarter-finals of the World Cup where he played on the left of a back three. He won four England Under-21 caps.

On his 21st birthday in 1994 he played on the left wing in Vienna, coming back from injury, as an injury-wrecked and young Chelsea side heroically drew 1–1 with Austria Memphis to win the European Cup Winners' Cup tie. But he missed the European quarter-final with Real Betis in Spain in 1998 because his girlfriend was giving birth to their son.

37.

Glorious and Less Glorious Debuts

The first Chelsea player to score on his debut was James Robertson in the 1–0 win at Leicester Fosse in September 1905.

Les Fridge, a 17-year-old youth team goalkeeper, conceded five goals on his only appearance in the first team: a 5–1 defeat at home to Watford in May 1986. That figure was equalled by Michael Pinner in a 4–5 home defeat by Wolves in April 1962.

Goalkeepers Arthur Robinson (0–6 v Preston, September 1908) and Stanley MacIntosh (2–6 v Derby, December 1930) both conceded six on their debuts.

Paul Canoville became Chelsea's first black player when he made his debut against Crystal Palace in April 1982.

Ian Hamilton was the youngest ever Chelsea player to make his debut. At the age of 16 years and 139 days he scored in a 1–1 draw at Tottenham on March 1967.

Graham Rix made his Chelsea debut against Viktoria Zizkov in September 1994 at the age of 36 years and 327 days, and so became Chelsea's oldest new boy.

The first Chelsea player to make his debut as a substitute was Roger Wosahlo against Stoke in April 1967. It was his only appearance for the club.

Paul Elliott and Joe Allon both scored debut goals on the opening day of the 1991/92 season in a 2–2 draw against Wimbledon.

Nigel Spackman scored after three minutes of his Chelsea debut in August

1983. In a further 266 games for the club, he scored just 13 more goals.

Charlie Cooke made his Chelsea debut in the semi-final of the Inter-Cities Fairs Cup against Barcelona in May 1965.

James Toomer and Frank Wolff played their only first team games in an FA Cup tie against Crystal Palace in November 1905. The regular first-choice players were fulfilling a League fixture on the same day.

Of the 51 goalkeepers to play for Chelsea, only 11 have kept clean sheets on their debut. They are Ronald Brebner, Jack Whitley, Colin Hampton, Frank Higgs, Vic Woodley, William Gibb Robertson, Peter Bonetti, Alex Stepney, Petar Borota, Eddie Niedzwiecki and Dave Beasant.

Outfield players Bob Mackie and David Webb both kept clean sheets on their one appearance starting in goal.

Alex Stepney is the only goalkeeper to keep a clean sheet on his debut and never play for the first team again.

Paul Williams made his Chelsea debut against Oldham Athletic in April 1983. The following weekend he competed in the London Marathon.

Harry Wilding was signed by Chelsea in April 1914 but because of the intervention of the First World War he had to wait over four years to make his debut. He then scored in a 3–2 win over Everton.

James Bradshaw scored in each of his first three matches for Chelsea in 1909, but played just three more games and never played League football again for any other club.

George Hilsdon scored five goals on his debut in a 9–2 win over Glossop North End in September 1906. This remains a Football League record.

Seamus O'Connell scored a hat-trick on his debut against Manchester United in October 1954. The visitors still won 6–5.

Joey Jones was sent off on his debut at Carlisle United in October 1983.

Billy Sinclair and James Smart made their only appearance for Chelsea at

Burnley in April 1964, the day after eight first team players were sent home after a fracas at the club's hotel in Blackpool. Chelsea lost the game 6–2.

Colin Court and Cliff Huxford made their debuts in Chelsea's first ever European tie, away to Frem Copenhagen in September 1958. It was to be Court's only appearance.

The first game of four consecutive seasons in the 1990s saw goals by Chelsea debutants. The marksmen were Paul Elliott and Joe Allon (1991/92), Mick Harford (1992/93), Gavin Peacock (1993/94), and Paul Furlong (1994/95).

Jimmy Clare, Steve Livingstone, Gerry Peyton and Roger Wosahlo all made their Chelsea debuts as substitutes and never played for the first team again.

Chris Hutchings, David Lee, Joe Allon, Eddie Newton, Paul Hughes and Tore Andre Flo all scored on their debuts having come on as substitute.

In April 1987 goalkeeper Roger Freestone made his debut and John Coady scored in his first start, away to Queens Park Rangers. In the corresponding fixture six years later, goalkeeper Dmitri Kharine made his debut and John Spencer scored in his first start.

Colin West scored within five minutes of his debut in Chelsea's 1–0 win over Arsenal at Stamford Bridge in March 1987.

Four players made their debuts on the opening day of the 1983/84 season in the 5–0 home win over Derby County. They were Eddie Niedzwiecki, Joe McLaughlin, Nigel Spackman and Kerry Dixon. The team went on to win the Second Division Championship.

John Boyle and Laurent Charvet both made their debuts in the semi-finals of the League Cup – Boyle in 1965 and Charvet in 1998.

Nils Middelboe became Chelsea's first foreign star when he made his debut in November 1913.

Craig Burley made his debut as a substitute in the 7–0 defeat by Nottingham Forest in April 1991.

Bryan 'Pop' Robson was aged 36 years 296 days when he scored the winning goal on his debut away to Cambridge United in August 1982. Until Rix, he was Chelsea's oldest debutant.

38.

Not just any Goal

Alan Hudson's goal against Ipswich on 26 September 1970 didn't enter the net. The 20 yard shot struck the side netting and spun back on to the pitch and amazingly the referee awarded the goal. Chelsea won 2–1.

Ben Howard Baker is Chelsea's only goalkeeper to score for the club. It was a penalty in November 1921 when the Blues beat Bradford City 1–0 at Stamford Bridge.

The youngest player to score for Chelsea was Ian Hamilton. He headed Chelsea's goal on his debut in the 1–1 draw at Tottenham in March 1967 when he was 16 years, 4 months and 18 days old.

When Eddie Newton scored in the 1997 FA Cup Final he created a club record. Including own goals as one entry, he became the 19th Chelsea goalscorer of the season.

Chelsea's all-time top five goalscorers are Bobby Tambling (202), Kerry Dixon (193), Roy Bentley and Peter Osgood (150) and Jimmy Greaves (132).

Peter Osgood scored in every round of the FA Cup success in 1970. He is still the last player to have achieved this feat.

Chelsea's second goal in the 3–1 win over Leicester at Stamford Bridge in December 1954 was officially recorded as a Froggatt and Milburn shared own goal. This is the only shared goal in the history of the Football League.

Chelsea's first League goal was scored in their second match by John Tait Robertson in the 1–0 win at Blackpool in September 1905.

Peter Osgood and David Webb scored in the 1970 Cup Final replay victory over Leeds at Old Trafford.

Mark Stein scored nine goals in seven consecutive games between December 1993 and February 1994. It still stands as a Premier League scoring sequence record.

Jimmy Greaves holds the club record for most goals in a season with a total of 43 goals in 1960/61.

The fastest recorded Chelsea goal is 13 seconds by Ben Whitehouse against Blackburn in December 1907.

Paul Canoville scored a goal after 11 seconds at the start of the second half at Sheffield Wednesday in the 4–4 draw in the Milk Cup in 1985. He had only just come on as substitute.

Graham Roberts scored 13 penalties in the Second Division Championship season in 1988/89.

Clive Walker scored arguably one of Chelsea's most important goals at Bolton in May 1983. By winning this match Chelsea avoided relegation to the old Third Division.

George Hilsdon scored 14 goals for England in only eight appearances between 1908 and 1909.

Gianfranco Zola's goal for Italy at Wembley in February 1997 was the first to be scored by a current Chelsea overseas player against England.

Australian-born Frank Mitchell was the first overseas player to score for Chelsea, in the 1–1 draw at Aston Villa in March 1949.

Prior to France '98, no player has never scored in a World Cup Finals tournament while on the Chelsea books.

On completion of his hat-trick against Manchester City in November 1960, Jimmy Greaves scored his 100th League goal for Chelsea before he had reached the age of 21 and is the youngest player ever to do so.

Bobby Tambling scored the consolation goal in the 1967 FA Cup Final 2–1 defeat by Tottenham.

38. Not just any Goal

Peter Houseman became the first Chelsea player to score as a substitute after replacing Peter Osgood in the 5–2 win against Charlton in the League Cup in 1966.

In Chelsea's 1971 Cup Winners' Cup success in Piraeus, Peter Osgood scored in the 1–1 draw with Real Madrid and again with John Dempsey in the 2–1 replay victory.

In Chelsea's only League Championship season in 1954/55 Roy Bentley was the team's leading scorer with 21 goals.

In Chelsea's two Second Division Championship seasons, Kerry Dixon was leading scorer on both occasions – scoring 34 in 1983/84 and 28 in 1988/89.

On 1 February 1992 Vinnie Jones and Dennis Wise scored in Chelsea's only League win at Liverpool since 1935.

During Chelsea's recent good run at Old Trafford, losing just twice since 1965, five Manchester United players have scored own goals: Pat Crerand (1966), Gary Walsh (1987), Gary Pallister (1990), Mal Donaghy (1992) and Henning Berg (1997).

When Roy Bentley and Bobby Smith both scored two on the last day of the 1950/51 season against Bolton, Chelsea avoided relegation to the old Second Division by 0.044 of a goal.

Peter Sillet scored 34 goals between 1955 and 1961 from full-back.

When Alan Mayes scored to put Chelsea 2–0 up against Bolton on 7 March 1981, little did he realize the next player to score would be Colin Lee on 29 August when Chelsea beat Bolton, again 2–0, 14½ playing hours later.

Arsenal's only defeat in their Championship season of 1990/91 was by Chelsea in February 1991. Graham Stuart and Kerry Dixon scored the goals.

Oh yes, and Roberto Di Matteo's 43 second goal against Middlesbrough was the quickest ever in a Wembley FA Cup Final. Gianfranco Zola won the European Cup Winners' Cup with his goal 17 seconds after coming on as substitute.

39.

Gustavo Poyet

Gustavo played in Real Zaragoza's victorious team over Chelsea in Spain in the 1995 European Cup Winners' Cup semi-final tie but missed the away leg, which Chelsea won, through suspension. He was booked in the first leg for a handball.

As well as winning the Cup Winners' Cup in 1995, he was a member of Uruguay's victorious Copa America team and was voted into the team of the tournament.

In his last four seasons at Zaragoza he scored 47 goals, and 80% of them were with his head. All this from midfield!

In his first 12 games with Chelsea he scored four goals. Only one was a header, a late winner against Newcastle. At Liverpool he scored a penalty in his 12th game.

Following that game he suffered a ruptured cruciate ligament when his studs caught in the ground during training. It was the first serious injury of his career.

Gustavo is 30 years old. He played for two years with Grenoble in France and for seven with Real Zaragoza. He is married with two children.

He was Chelsea's second signing under the free transfer 'Bosman' rule. Frode Grodås was the first.

His knee was mended by the same Belgian surgeon who operated on Ruud Gullit's knee during the latter years of the Dutchman's career. He was fit to score on his first start six months later and then won a European Cup Winners' Cup medal.

40.

Celestine Babayaro

Celestine left home in Kaduna, Nigeria, at the age of 15 to join Anderlecht in Belgium. Within one year he was in the first team.

A series of injuries plagued his first year at Chelsea. He suffered from a bad groin strain and two stress fractures of the foot.

He succeeded Daniel Amokachi who had moved to Everton as winner of the Best African in Belgium award in 1996. He was still only 18 years old.

At the age of 16 he won the Belgian League Championship. The following year he won his Olympic gold medal.

The first time Chelsea enquired as to his availability Anderlecht wanted £4.25m. When Chelsea went back several months later when there was only a year left on his contract the price had dropped. His £2.25m move was a Chelsea record for a teenager.

Mostly used at left wing-back by Anderlecht and Nigeria, he has also man-marked and played in a variety of positions up and down the left. In the quarter-finals of the UEFA Cup in 1996 he man-marked Inter Milan's Djorkaeff out of the game while playing for Anderlecht.

He lives in Acton, has a strong Catholic faith and attends church every Sunday.

He was ever present in the Nigeria side which became the first to qualify for the 1998 World Cup.

41.

Keeping up Appearances

Defender David Webb was forced to start a game in goal when he played a full match at home to Ipswich on Boxing Day 1971. Peter Bonetti and John Phillips were injured and Steve Sherwood arrived late due to fog. Webb kept a clean sheet in Chelsea's 2–0 win.

Since the formation of the Premier League, no player has played throughout the League season in every game. The last time this occurred was in 1989/90 when both Dave Beasant and Kerry Dixon were ever present in the old First Division.

Steve Clarke made his 400th appearance for the club at Ipswich in the Coca-Cola Cup in January 1998, the eighth player to do so.

Danish born Nils Middelboe, who made 46 appearances between 1913 and 1921, was Chelsea's first foreign international.

Chelsea's all-time top five appearance makers at the end of 1997/8 were Ron Harris (795), Peter Bonetti (729), John Hollins (592), Steve Clarke (421), Kerry Dixon (420), Eddie McCreadie (410) and John Bumstead (409).

Muzzy Izzet became the first player not to make a first team appearance for the club to be transferred for a fee; £800,000 to Leicester in July 1996.

In 1996/97 five goalkeepers made an appearance in Chelsea's goal. They were Dmitri Kharine, Kevin Hitchcock, Frode Grodås, Nick Colgan and Craig Forrest on loan.

Goalkeeper Les Fridge made only one appearance, a 5–1 home defeat by Watford on the last day of the 1985/86 season.

Dick Spence, at 39 years, one month and 26 days became the oldest first-team player in Chelsea history when he made his 246th and final appearance at home to Bolton on 13 September, 1947.

Ron Harris has made the most appearances as captain of Chelsea since the Second World War with a total of 322.

Goalkeeper Peter Bonetti has kept the most clean sheets in a season. In 48 appearances in 1971/72 he managed 21 shut-outs.

Dave Beasant has made the longest unbroken run by a goalkeeper. He appeared in 84 successive games between January 1989 and October 1990.

Ruud Gullit's 64th and final appearance was at Arsenal in the first leg of the Coca-Cola Cup semi-final on 28 January 1998.

Graham Rix, then 36 years, ten months and 23 days became the oldest player to make his first team debut when he was an 89th minute substitute against Viktoria Zizkov at home in the European Cup Winners' Cup on 15 September 1994.

John Hollins holds the Chelsea record for consecutive appearances with 168 from 14 August 1971 to 25 September 1974.

Steve Livingstone's only appearance was at Old Trafford in April 1993 when he played the last 35 minutes as a substitute for Neil Shipperley. Manchester United won 3–0.

Three other players who have left the club made only one appearance as substitute. They were Jimmy Clare (1980), goalkeeper Gerry Peyton on loan from Everton (1993) and Roger Wosahlo (1967).

Two loan goalkeepers have each played three games for the Blues. Craig Forrest, on loan from Ipswich in April 1997, was one, and Perry Digweed, on loan from Brighton, was the other.

Jack Harrow, who played 333 games for the club, had to retire in 1926 when his eyesight was impaired after the ball hit him in the face.

41. Keeping up Appearances

On Peter Osgood's 61st appearance on 5 October 1966 he broke his leg in a League Cup tie at Blackpool. He went on to play 380 games.

David Lee has made the most appearances as substitute. At the end of 1997/8 the total stood at 46.

The first penalty awarded against Chelsea was saved on his and Chelsea's first game by Bill Foulke at Stockport in September 1905. Despite his efforts Chelsea still lost 1–0.

Ron Harris is the only person ever to have appeared in a Cup Final captaining a winning side, a losing side and a team which has drawn.

42.

Safety in Numbers

Stamford Bridge's first League gate was 6,000 for the 5–1 Second Division win over Hull City in September 1905. This was followed by 20,000 for the visit of West Bromwich later that month.

67,000 turned out for Manchester United at Easter in that first season. The game finished 1–1.

A new record was established in the relegation season of 1909/10 when 70,000 witnessed the 2–1 win over Newcastle on 27 December – the largest crowd to watch a League match up to that time.

The Blues' lowest average League gate was 12,672 for 1982/83, when the team was almost relegated to the old Division Three.

The official record attendance is 82,905 for the visit of Arsenal on 12 October 1935 – the second largest club record gate in the Football League.

The visit of Moscow Dynamo for a friendly in November 1945 probably drew many thousands more, but a large proportion of those had entered the ground unofficially. The official attendance was 74,496.

Chelsea have had the highest average attendance in a League season on ten occasions (the same number as Newcastle United): 1907/8, 1909/10, 1911/12, 1912/13, 1913/14, 1919/20, 1921/22, 1923/24, 1925/26 and 1954/55.

Only Manchester United, Everton and Arsenal have had more appearances at the top of the average attendance list.

Only nine different clubs have finished with the highest average League attendance. Apart from the five already mentioned, Aston Villa, Liverpool, Tottenham Hotspur and Manchester City have also done so.

Chelsea were the first team to average home attendances of over 40,000 in one season, with an average of 42,615 in 1919/20.

The club has averaged over 40,000 at home in the League on ten occasions: 1919/20, 1946/47, 1947/48, 1948/49, 1949/50, 1952/53, 1953/54, 1954/55, 1958/59 and 1969/70.

Chelsea's highest average League crowd was 48,260 for the Championship season of 1954/55.

The Blues were also the first team to top the average attendance chart when in the Second Division – 26,295 in 1911/12. The club managed that feat once more, averaging 32,355 in 1925/26.

Chelsea did not fall out of the top ten for average League attendances until 1956/57, when the Blues had the eleventh best League average, with 31,732.

It only happened once more (1961/62) before 1972/73, when Chelsea averaged 29,722, the 12th best attendance record in the League.

Since then, Chelsea have slipped behind in the attendance chart, only regaining a top ten place in 1996/97, averaging 27,620 (over 2,000 less than relegated Middlesbrough). However, times could be a-changing!

In 1997/98 Chelsea rose to eighth place in the Premier League average attendances with 33,333, the club's highest number since 1971/72.

Only eight clubs have finished in the top ten for average League attendances on more occasions than Chelsea: Everton, Liverpool, Newcastle, Aston Villa, Manchester United, Arsenal, Manchester City and Tottenham.

Chelsea have finished best supported club in Division Two on eight occasions: 1906/07, 1910/11, 1911/12, 1924/25, 1925/26, 1928/29, 1929/30 and 1976/77.

Chelsea's lowest position in the average attendance chart was 28th, in 1981/82 (average 13,132).

Chelsea's average home League attendance (29,722) did not fall below the average of the division they played in until 1972/73 — a run of 56 years.

In 1981/82, Sheffield United of the old Fourth Division averaged 14,892, almost 2,000 more than Second Division Chelsea, with 13,132.

The largest post-war attendance at the Bridge remains the 77,696 who watched a League game on 16 October 1948. Chelsea drew 3–3 with Blackpool.

The smallest post-war League attendance came on 5 May 1982, when just 6,009 paid to see the Division Two match against Orient.

That same season, just 3,935 watched Chelsea play at Wrexham on 27 February 1982.

The crowd of 77,952 for the FA Cup fourth round tie (the equivalent of today's sixth round) with Southern League Swindon on 13 March 1911, remains the largest for that competition at Stamford Bridge and was then a record for any competition at the ground.

The smallest attendance for an FA Cup tie at Stamford Bridge was approximately 5,000, for the visit of 1st Grenadiers on 7 October 1905.

The highest attendance for a League Cup tie at the Bridge came on 22 December 1971, when 43,330 watched the first leg of the semi-final against Tottenham. Chelsea won 3–2.

The smallest League Cup crowd at the Bridge was 5,630 for the visit of Workington Town on 24 October 1960. Chelsea won 4–2.

59,541 saw the Inter-Cities Fairs Cup tie against AC Milan on 16 February 1966, the largest gate for a European tie at the Bridge. Chelsea won 2–1.

The smallest crowd for a European tie was 13,104 for the visit of Danish team Frem in the Fairs Cup on 4 November 1958 — Chelsea's first ever European tie.

The largest crowd for a Chelsea away match (not including Wembley Stadium) is the 70,000 who went to the Fairs Cup semi-final first leg match at the Nou Camp on 27 April 1966. Barcelona won 2–0.

42. Safety in Numbers

The largest crowd for an away match featuring Chelsea in Britain is 68,386 for the League match at Newcastle on 3 September 1930. It was Hughie Gallacher's second game for Chelsea, his first return to Newcastle from where Chelsea had bought him, and the crowd figure remains a Newcastle record.

43.

The Firm: Chelsea Village plc

Chelsea Village is the holding company of Chelsea Football Club and the other principal businesses.

The other businesses are Chelsea Village Hotel, Chelsea Village Catering, Chelsea Village Merchandising (which is the merchandising of Chelsea products through the Megastore and mail order), Chelsea Village Communications and Elizabeth Duff Travel.

Chelsea Village has five directors: Ken Bates and Michael Russell, who are executive, and three non-executive, who are Patrick Murrin, Mark Taylor and Stewart Thompson.

Executive directors are effectively employed by the group, non-executive ones give an overview and look after the good and proper management of the group.

Ken Bates is chairman and Michael Russell is finance director. Russell joined after four years as finance director of London Transport Property.

Patrick Murrin is a chartered accountant who looks after a substantial shareholding on behalf of Swan Management. Mark Taylor is a solicitor specializing in company and commercial law and represented Chelsea in the latter stages of the battle to save Stamford Bridge. Stewart Thompson is a long-time Chelsea supporter and chief executive of one of the biggest single sachet sugar companies in Europe.

Chelsea Village is the group banker and therefore the banker to the football club. Chelsea Village applies financial discipline to Chelsea Football Club through the budgeting process.

Chelsea Village Catering has eight function rooms throughout Stamford

43. The Firm: Chelsea Village plc

Bridge operating seven days a week: Bentley's, Drake's, Ossie's, Tambling's, Dixon's, the Trophy Room, the Galleria and Midnight At Chelsea.

Half of Chelsea Village Catering's revenue is derived from non-match days.

Functions encompass a wide area from product launches to weddings.

Chelsea Village Merchandising went from nothing to a multi-million pound business in the space of nine months.

Chelsea Village Hotel has 160 bedrooms of four-star quality and a restaurant — the King's Brasserie which serves contemporary New York food.

Three restaurants stand under the hotel: Fish Nets, The Shed Bar and Arkle's, an Irish restaurant.

The fully staffed hotel employs 64 people.

Chelsea Village, excluding the hotel and restaurant, employs 141 people.

Chelsea Football Club employs 66 people, including players, trainees and administration.

Chelsea Village is listed on the Stock Exchange under the Alternative Investments Market. There are in excess of 12,000 shareholders.

Chelsea Football Club directors are Ken Bates, Colin Hutchinson and Yvonne Todd.

Chelsea Village was quoted by the *Financial Times* in January 1998 as being one of the 500 top companies in the UK.

When the development site is complete it will house 54 flats.

The underground car park offers 234 spaces.

'Chelsea Village's vision is to make itself the premier sports and leisure group in the country,' says Ken Bates, 'providing a stage for a team to rank among the best in Europe.'

The finance is in place to complete all the development plans in their entirety.

A Stamford Bridge wedding party which took place the week after the team won the Cup in 1997 was lined up in front of the Matthew Harding Stand for the classic picture. The South Stand had development hoardings up. Clothes suddenly started appearing over them, and a man appeared, dressed only in his socks, and did a lap of the pitch.

44.

The Directors

Throughout its 93 year history Chelsea Football Club has had 43 directors serving on the board, seven being the largest number to hold office at any one time (in the first two seasons) and three the smallest (as at the present time).

Longest serving of all was Mr Claude W Kirby who held office for 30 years (1905–1935), and was chairman throughout this time until his death.

Peter Middleton, chief executive of Lloyds of London was the shortest-serving director, being a member of the board for a few months in 1996.

Colonel Crisp was the second chairman of Chelsea FC, holding office from 1935 until the early days of the Second World War. A one-time mayor of Lewes, he was instantly recognizable with his walrus moustache and black bowler hat.

For 78 years (1905–1983) the Mears family had at least one representative on the board. JT Mears (the club's founder) and HA Mears were the first and David Mears the last of seven members of the family.

Although, by tradition, the Earls of Cadogan were Presidents of Chelsea FC, and held that office from 1905–1983, they were never members of the board. The son of the late Lord Cadogan, Viscount Chelsea, was, however, a director from 1964–1983, and chairman from 1981 to 1982.

Probably the most famous of all Chelsea directors from other spheres of life was Sir Richard Attenborough CBE, the well known actor and director who was a director from 1969–82.

The only ex-Chelsea player to be a member of the board was Vivian Woodward, the famous amateur footballer, who represented England at both professional and amateur level (66 caps), and who played for Chelsea from 1909–15. He was on the board from 1922 until his death in 1930.

Another long-serving family on the Chelsea board was the Pratts (father and son). C J Pratt senior served from 1922 to 1936 (chairman in his last year), while CJ junior was director from 1935 to 1968 (chairman in his last two years).

The present chairman of Wimbledon Football Club, Mr Stanley Reed, was a member of the Chelsea board of directors from 1981 to 1982.

The only ex-manager to be appointed to the board of directors, who served immediately after standing down as manager, was Mr John Neal from 1985 to 1986.

Martin Spencer was another to have two separate spells on the board, from 1977 to 1978 and 1980 to 1983, holding the office of chief executive in the interim.

George Thomson, a director from 1968 to 1982, succeeded the second Earl Cadogan as President of Chelsea FC in 1983, having previously been given the title of Life Vice-President. He was President until the time of his death in 1996.

Ken Bates was appointed to the board of directors in 1981, succeeding to the chairmanship the following year. After Claude Kirby and Brian Mears, he is now Chelsea's third-longest serving chairman.

Yvonne Todd is the first female member of the Chelsea FC board of directors.

45.

Stamford Bridge
Is Building Up

When the stadium at Stamford Bridge was developed in 1876, it was not built for football but for athletics by the London Athletic Club.

The eight-and-a-half acre site that contained an orchard and a market garden was cleared in a few months and the ground was opened on 28 April 1877.

The ground became the property of Gus Mears, wealthy son of a building contractor, in 1904 when the former freeholder died. His aim – to turn it into a major football stadium.

Fulham refused Gus Mears' offer to play home games at the Bridge for £1,500 a year.

Renowned and much-used architect Archibald Leitch was commissioned to design the new ground. It included a 120-yard long stand on the east side to hold 5,000 spectators, with three open sides built on thousands of tons of soil and clay excavated during the construction of the Piccadilly tube line.

Stamford Bridge was then the second largest ground in the country behind Crystal Palace, the FA Cup Final venue.

Stamford Bridge hosted three FA Cup Finals between 1920 and 1922, all with a 1–0 result. Unfortunately for Blues supporters, Spurs won the Cup at their home in 1921.

The 1922 Final between Preston North End and Huddersfield Town was the first to be decided by a penalty. Huddersfield won 1–0.

The ground has also hosted ten FA Cup semi-finals (the last in 1978), ten

Charity Shield matches, four Amateur Cup Finals and four full England internationals.

No additional seating capacity was added to the ground until 1939, with the building of the infamous North Stand, also designed by Leitch, which stood on stilts above the terracing. It was not used until October 1945 and was demolished in 1975.

Not only did athletics continue at the stadium but it has hosted a variety of sports over the years: speedway, greyhound racing, cricket, rugby league, rugby union, baseball and midget car racing.

The south terrace roofing which in 1966 gave that section of the ground its name – the Shed – was erected in the mid-1930s to provide cover for the bookmakers on dog racing nights. This too was designed by Leitch, becoming known at first as 'Leitch's Folly'.

Floodlights were installed in the 1950s and made their debut for a friendly against Sparta Prague on 19 March 1957. There were six towers, each 170ft high.

The first West Stand was built between 1964 and 1965; it cost £150,000 and included over 6,000 seats. More than 3,000 bench seats were later installed at the front.

Some claim the removal of the weather vane, modelled on centre-forward George Hilsdon, from the old East Stand by chairman Brian Mears in the 1970s, was responsible for the mixture of bad luck and bad management that threw Chelsea into crisis in the 1970s and 1980s. A copy was restored to the ground in the early 1980s and moved to the West Stand in 1983. It is now above the East Stand again.

The new East Stand, designed by Darbourne and Darke, at a cost of £2m, was begun in 1973 and opened for the first game of the 1974/75 season – one year behind schedule.

The last game in front of the old North Terrace was against Manchester City on 22 November 1993.

The last game in front of the Shed terrace was against Sheffield United on

45. Stamford Bridge Is Building Up

7 May 1994. Chelsea scored in the last minute to win 3–2 and condemn United to relegation.

The first game in front of the temporary Shed seating was against Norwich on 20 August 1994. The seating took 3,624.

The new North Stand opened on 26 November 1994 for a match against Everton with a capacity for the day of 5,200 – this was soon to rise to 8,200.

The North Stand was renamed the Matthew Harding Stand in the wake of the millionaire director's death in a helicopter crash on 22 October 1996.

Work on removing the roof of the old West Stand began in April 1997 and it was demolished that summer, with work starting on the new stand straight away. Spectators were allowed to sit in the still developing lower tier of the new stand for the first game of the 1997/98 season.

Chelsea's home fixtures for 1997/98 were delayed as finishing touches were made to the Shed End Stand. It was opened for a match with Southampton on 30 August 1997.

46.

Importing Quality

Danish international half-back Nils Middleboe retained his amateur status throughout his link with Chelsea (1913–21), reputedly refusing even to claim expenses. He played a total of 46 games.

Swiss international defender Willi Steffen played 20 games for the Blues in 1946/47 whilst visiting Britain. He had been a fighter pilot in the Swiss air force.

South African centre-half Ralph Oelofse played just eight League games for the Blues between March and September 1952 before moving on to Watford in July 1953.

Durban-born South African Derek Smethurst, who played just 19 games for the Blues in the early 1970s, scored the goal that beat Manchester City in the first leg of the European Cup Winners' Cup semi-final on 14 April 1971, and came on as a sub for Peter Osgood in the final against Real Madrid.

South African-born Colin Viljoen, who made 23 appearances for Chelsea in the very early 1980s, took up British nationality in 1971. He had a distinguished career with Ipswich and Manchester City, and won two England caps in 1975.

Yugoslav international goalkeeper Petar Borota, with the Blues between 1978 and 1982, holds the record for clean sheets in a League season – he kept 18.

England international Tony Dorigo, who played for Chelsea between 1987 and 1991, was actually born in Melbourne, Australia. He was relegated two seasons running, with Aston Villa in 1987 and Chelsea in 1988.

Dutch centre-half Ken Monkou was the first black player to become Chelsea Player of the Year when he won the award in 1990.

46. Importing Quality

Signed for £306,000 in late 1989, Norwegian international Erland Johnsen made 173 appearances for Chelsea, scoring just once. He won a Full Members' Cup winners' medal in 1990 and an FA Cup runners-up medal in 1994.

Danish international Jakob Kjeldbjerg was forced to retire in December 1996 at the age of 27 after an 18-month lay-off with a knee injury. He won an FA Cup runners-up medal in 1994. He still lives in England and works for Danish television.

Russian international keeper Dmitri Kharine became the first current Blues player to captain his country in the World Cup when he led Russia in the United States in 1994.

Kharine has a higher percentage of clean sheets than any other goalkeeper who has played over 100 games.

Kharine has also won an Olympic gold medal with Russia, who beat Brazil 2–1 in the 1988 Seoul football tournament.

Ruud Gullit is the most honoured player to appear for Chelsea. In Holland the Dutchman won three Dutch League championships and one Dutch Cup, and he was Dutch Footballer of the Year twice. In Italy he won two European Cups, one World Club championship, one European Super Cup, three Italian championships, one Italian Cup and two Italian Super Cups. For Holland he captained the 1988 European Championship winning side, being named second best player in the tournament, and won a total of 65 Dutch caps. He was also World and European Footballer of the Year in 1987.

Despite coming before the Bosman case which made out of contract players a free transfer, Gullit was signed on a free transfer in June 1995. He had a free transfer at the end of his Sampdoria contract written into it when he signed.

Romanian international Dan Petrescu won four League Championships and two Romanian Cups with Steaua Bucharest between 1986 and 1989.

When Petrescu was signed in November 1995, it was for a club record-equalling fee of £2.3m.

Italian international midfielder Roberto Di Matteo became Chelsea's record purchase in July 1996 when he signed from Lazio for £4.9m.

Di Matteo was born in Shaffhausen, Switzerland, but qualifies for Italy through parentage.

French international Frank Leboeuf was signed for a then club record fee of £2.5m in June 1996. The record lasted two days until Di Matteo's arrival.

Leboeuf made the French squad for Euro '96 in England, but did not play in any of France's five matches.

Manager Gianluca Vialli won the following honours as a player in Italy: a League Championship, three Italian Cups, the European Cup Winners' Cup and the Italian Super Cup whilst with Sampdoria; the European Cup (as captain), the UEFA Cup, the League, the Italian Cup and the Italian Super Cup whilst with Juventus; and 59 Italian caps. He has played in two World Cups and one European Championship.

Vialli joined Chelsea on a free transfer in May 1996. Like Gullit, it was before Bosman.

When he was named Premiership Footballer of the Year in 1997, Gianfranco Zola became the first Chelsea player to win the award. And he only joined the club in November 1996.

Norwegian international Tore Andre Flo is the younger brother of Jostein Flo, who played for Sheffield United.

Tore Andre scored a hat-trick in his last game for SK Brann Bergen before joining Chelsea, and has scored a hat-trick for Norway against the United Arab Emirates.

Signed from Anderlecht in June 1997 for £2.25m when still just 18, Celestine Babayaro is Chelsea's record teenage signing. The previous record was £350,000 for Anthony Barness in 1992.

Babayaro was a regular in the Anderlecht side aged 16. He won a Belgian championship and the Belgian Cup, and was named Belgian Young Player of the Year twice.

46. Importing Quality

Like Dmitri Kharine, Babayaro has won an Olympic gold – in his case for Nigeria at the 1996 Atlanta football tournament. He scored in the final.

Uruguayan international midfielder Gustavo Poyet, currently with the Blues, holds dual Uruguayan and Spanish nationality, having spent seven years at Real Zaragoza.

Dutch international keeper Ed de Goey is the tallest man ever to play for Chelsea at 6ft 6in.

Frenchman Bernard Lambourde was born in Guadeloupe.

47.

Summer Travels '98

Chelsea's record purchase Pierluigi Casiraghi, signed at Stamford Bridge in a £5.4m move from Lazio. Lazio's President, Cragnotti tried to buy back Roberto Di Matteo as part of the deal but Chelsea wouldn't sell.

Casiraghi partnered Gianfranco Zola in attack when Italy beat England at Wembley in the 1998 World Cup qualifiers.

Brian Laudrup completed his signing for Chelsea on a Saturday lunchtime in Copenhagen just before reporting for World Cup duty.

Laudrup became Chelsea's second player to have won a European Champions medal with his country. The first was Ruud Gullit.

Albert Ferrer signed for Chelsea at Spain's World Cup headquarters in Chantille in France on the Monday evening after Landrup's signing. He cost £2.2m from Barcelona.

Ferrer was in the Barcelona team which defeated Sampdoria at Wembley in the 1992 European Cup Final. Gianluca Vialli was on the losing side.

Marcel Desailly signed for Chelsea at France's World Cup headquarters the day after Ferrer. He cost £4.6m from AC Milan.

Desailly won the European Cup two years running with different clubs: Marseilles in 1993 and Milan in 1994.

48.

Wonderful Servants: Testimonials

Physio Harry Medhurst and former player Dick Spence were granted a joint testimonial in March 1976.

Programme editor Hugh Hastings appeared as a second-half substitute at Brentford in a testimonial match for Eddie Lyons in May 1984.

Brazilian star Emerson was in the Porto line-up for the Paul Elliott benefit match in August 1995. He later played against Chelsea in the 1997 FA Cup Final for Middlesbrough.

Tommy Meehan and Peter Houseman are the two Chelsea players to receive posthumous benefit matches.

Of the 1970 FA Cup-winning team, only Tommy Baldwin and David Webb did not later receive a testimonial.

Peter Bonetti scored two penalties in the Bobby Tambling testimonial against Charlton in May 1968.

The highest crowd for a Chelsea player was the 20,949 who attended the Ken Shellito testimonial against QPR in May 1968.

Standard Liege of Belgium were the first overseas opponents for a testimonial – at Peter Bonetti's in May 1971.

England cricket captain Ian Botham played in the Ron Harris testimonial in April 1980.

Frank Blunstone, Micky Droy and Ian Hutchinson are the only Chelsea players to score in their own testimonial matches.

Peter Bonetti, Ron Harris and Ian Hutchinson have each received two testimonial matches.

Chelsea played in a testimonial for Fulham goalkeeper Gerry Peyton in May 1986. Peyton later played one League game as a substitute while on loan to Chelsea in January 1993.

Former goalkeeper Dave Beasant came on as a substitute centre-forward in the Kerry Dixon testimonial in March 1995 and scored in a 5–1 win over Tottenham Hotspur.

David Speedie was fined £700 by the Football Association for dropping his shorts during a testimonial match for Eddie Niedzwiecki in May 1989.

Augustus Harding was granted a testimonial in February 1913 after making just four League appearances in seven years at the club.

One of Chelsea's greatest ever goalscorers, George Hilsdon, had to share a benefit match with winger William Bridgeman. The pair shared receipts of £180 from the game played on Easter Monday 1912.

In December 1979, Chelsea played at Weymouth in a testimonial match for the non-League players Derek Courtney and Bryan Lawrence. Included in the Weymouth team was Graham Roberts, later a Chelsea captain.

Ray Wilkins' only appearance at Stamford Bridge for Manchester United was in the Peter Bonetti testimonial in September 1979.

John Dempsey played for Philadelphia Fury at the time of his testimonial match in February 1980.

The manager of the Chelsea Restaurant, Leon Lenik, made a second-half substitute appearance in the Micky Droy testimonial match, against Arsenal in November 1983.

One of the linesmen for the Kerry Dixon testimonial with Spurs in March 1995 was a Chelsea season-ticket holder, Perry Gascoine.

Chelsea played QPR at Stamford Bridge in May 1968 in a testimonial for Ken Shellito. Seven days later the two teams met at Loftus Road in a benefit for Mike Keen.

Chelsea played Southend in May 1990 in a testimonial match for Danny Greaves – son of the former Chelsea player, Jimmy Greaves.

Chelsea played Reading in a benefit match for Paul Canoville in August 1988. Canoville's career was ended by a serious knee injury after just nine games for Reading following his move from Chelsea.

49.

Friendlies

One of the most outstanding friendlies Chelsea ever played was against the New York Cosmos on 26 September 1978 when 39,659 people assembled at Stamford Bridge to witness a 1—1 draw that involved such names as Yashin, Beckenbauer, Cruyff and Chinaglia.

Chelsea's first ever friendly was against Liverpool at Stamford Bridge on 4 September 1905 with Chelsea 4—0 victors thanks to goals from Bob McRoberts (2), Martin Moran and Jimmy Windridge.

The most famous friendly was against Moscow Dynamo immediately after the war on 13 November 1945 with an official attendance of 74,496, but an estimated 100,000 (the gates were forced) watched a dramatic 3—3 draw.

Very few friendlies were played before 1915 and information is scarce about those that were. One on 21 February 1914 against Spurs was won 7—3 by the Blues, the goals coming from Bob Whittingham, Harry Ford (2), Harold Halse (3) and Harold Brittain.

Chelsea's first ever tour abroad was at the end of 1905/06 season, to Austria, Hungary and Denmark. Five matches were played, only three results are known — one was won and two were lost.

In 1906/07 a match was held between George Robey's XI and Chelsea, in aid of the dependants of Jimmy Miller, a club trainer, who died during that year. Music hall entertainer George scored a brilliant goal and was promptly registered to play for Chelsea in London League fixtures.

A two-match trip to Copenhagen in May 1919 against a combined Copenhagen team called Staevnet resulted in a 1—1 draw and a 2—1 defeat.

The first extensive tour was undertaken in May and June 1929 when nine matches were played in Buenos Aires, Sao Paulo, Rio and Montevideo. The record was: played 9, won 3, drew 2, lost 4, F 17, A 20.

A return to play Staevnet was made in 1938 when the Blues won both matches, 3–1 and 4–1 and a third game against UDV Danskhold (practically a national side) was won 2–0.

From 1947 a series of matches were played against Heart of Midlothian, home and away, on alternate years. A trophy was awarded in 1951 called the Stamford Bridge Cup. Eight matches were played, six were won, one drawn and one lost.

Another extensive tour was undertaken in April/May 1946 (a forerunner to many more in the following years) to Switzerland and Copenhagen once again. Eight matches were played, seven were won and the only defeat was in the first game 2–1 v KB Copenhagen. A good goals ratio of 30–6 was achieved.

A four-match tour to Algeria was made in May 1951, resulting in three victories and a draw. The goals record was F 8, A 2. Bobby Smith scored six goals.

A month-long tour to Dublin, Luxembourg, USA and Canada saw ten matches played against such worthy opponents as Rangers, Fortuna Dusseldorf, Borussia Dortmund and a couple of USA sides. The final record was: played 10, won 6, drew 2, lost 2, F 26, A13. Chelsea took a pounding from Borussia Dortmund to the tune of 6–1.

The 1954/55 season saw a dramatic match against Red Banner, later to change their name several times, to CDNA, CSKA and Sredets, on 15 December 1954 on a Wednesday afternoon before 40,452 people. An exciting 2–2 draw was fought out in very muddy conditions.

The first floodlit game was played at Stamford Bridge on 19 March 1957 against Sparta Prague. Chelsea won 2–0 in front of 30,701 spectators, the goals coming from Les Allen and Derek Gibbs.

On 7 November 1957 the Blues suffered a 4–1 home defeat at the hands of CDNA Moscow before 41,991 spectators. A week later they entertained Beogradski Yugoslavia and won 2–1 but only 11,513 attended. On 25 March 1958 against CDNA Sofia a 1–1 draw attracted 11,000 spectators.

A trip to Bulgaria in August 1958 saw the Blues play CDNA Sofia, losing 2–1, and then Levski Sofia, winning 2–0.

Two matches against Athletic Bilbao saw a 5–3 home victory and a 1–0 away defeat.

Another month-long tour was embarked on in May/June 1964 to the West Indies. A series of five matches against Wolves plus games against Barbados, Jamaica, Haiti and a couple of club sides were played. The series against Wolves resulted in: played 5, won 3, lost 2, F 10, A 9. Bobby Tambling finished with 16 goals.

Pre-season tours started to take off with a five-match tour to five different countries: Denmark, Sweden, Germany, Switzerland and Austria – in 1964.

The end of season tour of 1964/65 went even further than the pre-season trip by going to Australia and Tasmania. Eleven matches were played with a record of: won 9, drew 2, lost 0, F 47, A 7.

The pre-season tour of 1965/66 was to Germany and Sweden for six matches; the record was: won 2, drew 2, lost 2, F 13, A 6.

On 17 August 1965 in Essen, Chelsea played the West German national team in a pre-World Cup warm up and lost 3–2 with McCalliog and Bridges scoring.

The pre-season 1966/67 tour was to Germany, Switzerland and Scotland. Six matches were played with two won and four lost. It was followed at the end of the season by a tour to USA, Canada and Bermuda of ten matches. The Blues won seven, drew one and lost three, with a goal count of 16 for and three against. The leading scorers were Baldwin (7), Hateley (7), Tambling (8).

Top attraction of the 1966/67 season was Real Madrid, beaten 2–0 before 32,277 with Hollins and Hateley scoring.

1970/71's post-season four-match tour to Trinidad and El Salvador included two matches against Southampton, which Chelsea won 8–3 and 6–2. There were also victories over the national sides of El Salvador and Trinidad. Top scorer was Baldwin with seven goals.

49. Friendlies

In 1973/74 this was followed by another long-distance tour to Australia. The Blues played only six matches, winning five and losing one.

The pre-season trip to Holland and Germany in 1974 gave false hope for the coming season. The Blues lost to Feyenoord but beat Borossia Monchengladbach and Wuppertaler SV and played well. But Division One status was lost.

Another long tour in May 1977 to Norway, USA and Canada resulted in five wins and one defeat, with Finnieston and Garner the leading scorers with five and four respectively.

The days of the pre- and post-season long tours came to an end with just two matches in Sweden; a 1–1 draw against Kalmar FF and a 1–0 win over Malmo FF in July 1977.

A three match trip to Norway in May 1978 gained Chelsea three victories against Jerv, Voss and Hauger – of 2–0, 6–1, 4–1 respectively.

Nine pre-season friendlies in July/August 1986 in Wales, Ireland and England gave a record of six wins and three defeats. The defeats against Plymouth, Torquay and Palace were very depressing to witness!

50.

Would You Credit It!

In the club's first season in the League, 1905/06, Chelsea had the tenth highest average League gate in the country, with 13,370 – the second highest in Division Two.

The third preliminary round of the FA Cup competition in November 1905 coincided with a Football League Division Two game against Burnley at Stamford Bridge. The League ordered Chelsea to turn out their recognized first team in the latter fixture (won 1–0) and the reserves were beaten by Palace 1–7.

In Chelsea's second ever FA Cup game against Southern United on 18 October 1905, the right-back Robert Mackie played in goal.

During the 1908/09 season when there were far fewer internationals played and no World Cup or European Championships, Chelsea's Jimmy Windridge, Ben Warren and George Hilsdon amassed 20 caps between them.

It's a record. Chelsea's longest League game undefeated sequence is 27 matches, accumulated in Division Two during the 1988/89 season. The run lasted from 29 October until 8 April and consisted of 20 wins and only seven draws.

And another record. The Blues' longest home sequence undefeated in a League season is 21 matches. This was achieved in the 1976/77 season in Division Two and lasted from 21 August until the end of the season. There were a staggering 15 wins and just six draws.

Chelsea's record unbeaten run away from home is 13 games, again recorded in Division Two, throughout the 1988/89 season. Of the 13 matches, 11 were straight victories.

Chelsea's longest winning sequence in the League and Cup combined lasted for eight matches. Six were League wins and two were in the FA Cup. It was in the 1965/66 season, dating from 27 December until 12 February.

The club's longest winning sequence at home in the League occurred way back during the 1906/07 season. The team strung together ten straight victories between 1 September and 26 January.

The most League games in a season without a victory at home was recorded in the 1994/95 season. The team went 12 games without a victory. Seven were draws. It wasn't until Chelsea played Aston Villa at Stamford Bridge on 15 April that they recorded a 1–0 victory. This was their first since beating Ipswich Town on 23 October the previous year.

The team's most League wins in a season is 29 out of a possible 46 matches. This was accomplished during the 1988/89 season.

The most League wins at home in a season is an amazing 18 out of a total of 19 matches, achieved during the 1906/7 season.

Chelsea's most away League wins in a season was accomplished during the 1988/89 campaign. The team recorded 14 wins from a possible 23.

Chelsea first gave a Player of the Year award in 1967. The winner was Peter Bonetti.

Players that have won the Player of the Year award twice are: John Hollins (1970, 1971), David Webb (1969, 1972), Charlie Cooke (1968, 1975), Ray Wilkins (1976, 1977), and Pat Nevin (1984, 1987).

The players who won the Player of the Year award from 1988 until 1993 were all in their first full season with the team. They were Tony Dorigo in 1988, Graham Roberts in 1989, Ken Monkou in 1990, Andy Townsend in 1991, Paul Elliott in 1992 and Frank Sinclair in 1993.

The first time in Chelsea's history that they failed to score in the first three League fixtures of the season took place at the start of the 1996/97 season. Those fixtures were at home to Everton on 19 August, a 0–0 draw; away to Nottingham Forest four days later, another goalless draw; and a 2–0 defeat away to Middlesbrough on 26 August.

Dmitri Kharine's three clean sheets at the start of the 1996/97 season was a start of the season record for the club whilst in the top flight. The record, however, for the best number of clean sheets at the start of the season came during the 1911/12 season in Division Two. The first four games all had clean sheets. They were 0–0 draws with Stockport and Leeds and wins of 1–0 over Derby and 4–0 against Wolves.

Apart from winning the European Cup Winners' Cup with Zaragoza in 1995, Gustavo Poyet also holds a Copa America medal, having been in the Uruguay team which beat Brazil in a penalty shoot-out in the 1995 final.

Chelsea are second behind Ipswich in the list of clubs to have played at least ten European home games and remained unbeaten in them. At the end of 1997/98 the top three were Ipswich (25), Chelsea (23) and Bologna (18).

At one wedding shortly after Ruud Gullit became manager the entire male half of the party, including the groom, wore Ruud Gullit wigs.

The second ever wedding at Stamford Bridge saw the bride in the full Chelsea kit plus a veil.

One couple who got married at Stamford Bridge subsequently had a girl whom they named Zola.

Chelsea's worst defeat was at Wolves on 26 September 1953. Wolves won 8–1. Roy Bentley scored Chelsea's goal.

Centre-forward Roy Bentley played the last of his 367 games for Chelsea at home to Sheffield Wednesday on 19 September 1956 before moving to Fulham. He had scored the last of his then record 150 goals against Blackpool on 28 April that year. He captained the Championship winning side and won 12 England caps.

Also on the move was Ken Armstrong, who played the last of his 402 Chelsea games at right-half on 13 April 1957 at Blackpool. He held the League record appearances for Chelsea (362) until it was overtaken by Peter Bonetti and he gained one full England cap.

50. Would You Credit It!

Jimmy Greaves scored all five goals in Chelsea's 5–4 win at Preston on 19 December 1959.

Thirteen other people started a game in goal during Peter Bonetti's 19 year era as first-choice goalkeeper. They were: Reg Matthews, Errol McNally, John Dunn, Jim Barron, Mike Pinner, Kingsley Whiffen, Alex Stepney, Tommy Hughes, John Phillips, David Webb, Steve Sherwood, Bob Iles and Petar Borota.

Ouch! Both Clives, Walker and Allen, scored against Chelsea soon after leaving. In Allen's case it was on his debut for his next club West Ham. Clive Walker scored twice at Stamford Bridge for Sunderland in the Milk Cup semi-final of 1985 to eliminate Chelsea.

Prior to his appointment to the Chelsea board of directors Colin Hutchinson had held the post of chief executive at Wimbledon Football Club and Carlisle Football Club.

The 1988/89 season began under a cloud with the Stamford Bridge terraces being closed for the first five League fixtures – the highest attendance being a mere 8,858 during that time. This was as a result of crowd disturbances at the play-off fixture against Middlesbrough in the last match of the previous season.

Pat Nevin turned out for the first 20 minutes of Eddie Niedzwiecki's 1989 benefit match despite it being the Tuesday before he was playing in the FA Cup Final for Everton. Niedzwiecki had been forced to retire through injury.

Paul Elliott became club captain in 1993 but never kicked another ball. He had already suffered the injury which was to end his career.

Mark Hughes scored his first Chelsea goal in the Paul Elliott benefit match against Porto in 1995.

Scott Minto's 35 yard top corner special against Blackburn on 5 March 1997 was Chelsea's 5,000th League goal.

Tore Andre Flo was Chelsea's 76th player to score on his debut.

At the end of the 1997/98 season Chelsea had scored six or more goals in a game on 52 occasions.

Mark Hughes is one of five players to have scored an FA Cup Final goal against a team he has subsequently joined. He scored against Chelsea for Manchester United in 1994. The others are Kevin Keegan (Liverpool against Newcastle in 1974); Frank Stapleton (Arsenal against Man United in 1979); Terry Fenwick (QPR against Tottenham in 1982); and Norman Whiteside (Manchester United against Everton in 1985).

When Ken Bates was faced in 1992 with raising £16.5m over two decades to secure the freehold of Stamford Bridge from the Royal Bank of Scotland, he said: 'That'll be the price of a good left-back in 20 years' time.'

Since Chelsea's Golden Boot award was officially started in 1991/92 the player to score the most in a season has been Neil Shipperley who hit 47 in 1992/93, made up of 32 for the youth team, 14 for the reserves and one for the first team.

51.

Count the Bruises
in the League Cup

When Chelsea first won the League Cup in 1965, it was not a major competition. Not all the League clubs entered, and the final was over two legs at each team's ground. The winners did not qualify for Europe.

Chelsea first entered the competition in 1960, beating Millwall 7–1, Workington 4–2 and Doncaster 7–1 before losing to Portsmouth.

In victory year Peter Osgood made his debut in the quarter-final replay against Workington, scoring both goals in a 2–0 win, and John Boyle made his debut in the semi-final first leg, scoring the winner at Aston Villa. Boyle played in the final, Osgood did not.

Chelsea won the first leg of the final thanks to a memorable goal by Eddie McCreadie who was playing centre-forward due to others' injuries. He ran 80 yards before slipping the winner past Gordon Banks. Chelsea won 3–2.

In the second leg Tommy Docherty sent his team out to defend in what he saw as the continental style. Chelsea came away with a winning 0–0 draw and the boos of the Leicester fans ringing in their ears.

In 1967 Peter Osgood suffered a broken leg at Blackpool and in 1969 Peter Bonetti was knocked out by a brick thrown by a Carlisle fan. Chelsea ended up losing both ties.

In 1969, Leeds were defeated 2–0 in a replay at Stamford Bridge. Charlie Cooke and Alan Birchenall scored. Later that season Chelsea beat Leeds in an FA Cup replay – in the Final!

In 1971 the 2–1 defeat at Manchester United was at the hands of George Best who counts his winner as one of his best goals, mainly because he kept his feet having run from the halfway line when Ron Harris tried to amputate them! He went on to round Bonetti and score with, as far as Chelsea fans were concerned, horrible grace.

Chelsea's first Wembley League Cup Final came in 1972. The road there included a 6–0 replay away win at Bolton. Tommy Baldwin scored a hat-trick.

The semi-final win over Tottenham was dramatic. John Hollins hit a late penalty winner at home, and Alan Hudson's low cross from a wide free-kick sneaked into the far corner of the goal in the last minutes of the second leg to give Chelsea a 5–4 aggregate win.

They reached the semi-finals again the following season, but Norwich beat the Blues. Chelsea were useless at Stamford Bridge in a 2–0 defeat. The second leg was abandoned due to fog near the end with Norwich leading 3–2, but they won the replayed game.

In six of the next eight years Chelsea went out in the second round, the round in which they started. Defeats included a 6–2 replay at Stoke and a 1–0 debacle at Crewe.

While in the Second Division in 1983, First Division Leicester were beaten on a penalty shoot-out. It was Chelsea's first ever, and Eddie Niedzwiecki saved the first and last kicks he faced.

The fantastic three-game epic of 1984/85 against Sheffield Wednesday included the 4–4 replay draw at Hillsborough when Chelsea came from a 3–0 half-time deficit to lead 4–3 before Doug Rougvie conceded a penalty and a late equalizer.

The second replay saw David Speedie equalize a Wednesday 25 yarder when Pat Nevin crossed to the far post. Short Micky Thomas headed a last-minute corner, the first outswinger of the night, into the net for a suitably dramatic winner.

Chelsea lost the first leg of the semi-final to relegation-bound Sunderland when substitute Dale Jasper, on for broken elbow victim Joe McLaughlin, conceded two penalties.

The second leg saw desperate crowd trouble. Sunderland won 3–2.

51. Count the Bruises in the League Cup

Chelsea's image hit an all-time low.

A run of stupid and inexcusable consecutive defeats started in 1986: Cardiff away; Reading over two legs in the second round; Scunthorpe in the second round including a 4–1 away deficit, where the only goal was an own goal; and Scarborough over two legs, the second leg being lost after a 2–0 lead was turned into a 3–2 defeat.

At Portsmouth in 1990 the team came from 2–0 down with nine minutes to go to win 3–2. The man of the match had been awarded to Portsmouth's Warren Aspinall who still had time to concede a penalty, break his arm and be carried away as Dennis Wise equalized. Kevin Wilson scored the stoppage-time winner.

Another semi-final in 1991, another lamentable performance. Second Division Sheffield Wednesday won 2–0 at Stamford Bridge and cruised to Wembley.

More sorrowful performances followed with defeats against Second Division Tranmere, Stoke and Bolton. After the latter, vice-chairman Matthew Harding was killed as he flew home in a helicopter.

The competition kicked off in 1997 with doubts as to whether there would be European qualification for the winners. Chelsea fielded several players who weren't getting regular games and gave a couple of debuts to young-sters in the early rounds. Blackburn were beaten in a penalty shoot-out and Southampton, who had their first team out, were beaten by a Jody Morris 25 yarder three minutes from the end of extra-time. The quarter-final at Ipswich was also won in a penalty shoot-out.

Laurent Charvet made his debut in the semi-final as John Boyle had done 33 years before. But as in recent semi-finals, Chelsea were pathetic in the first leg at Arsenal and lost 2–1.

In between the two legs manager Ruud Gullit was dramatically released from his job, and Gianluca Vialli took charge for his first game. Chelsea hammered Arsenal 3–1 and reached their first League Cup Final for 26 years.

The final was the third meeting between Chelsea and Middlesbrough at

Wembley in the 1990s. Chelsea won all three games and didn't concede a goal.

Paul Gascoigne made his Middlesbrough debut in the final. His previous League Cup game was in 1991 for Tottenham when they got demolished by Chelsea 3-0 at White Hart Lane.